Improving Behaviour and Wellbeing in Primary Schools

This accessible resource provides a vivid and practical guide to social and emotional learning and will help primary schools tackle and improve behaviour and wellbeing. With content written by teachers and used successfully in real classrooms, chapters include powerful stories from teachers about their work and the impact it has had. Developed within a theoretical framework of evidence-based strategies, the resources included are fully illustrated with photographs from classrooms and draw upon a useful bank of downloadable resources and proformas. Taking the reader through a journey of how a group of schools worked together to develop practical and effective approaches, this essential resource features:

- Tried and tested strategies for improving behaviour and wellbeing
- Ready-to-use classroom resources – lesson slides; top picture-books for teaching about emotions; 20 simple exercises to help children stay calm; playground conflict resources and a progression in learning emotion vocabulary from Reception to Year 6
- Powerful stories from individual teachers about their work and its impact
- An in-depth understanding of research evidence on what works in tackling social, emotional and mental health needs from best-selling author and expert Jean Gross

Children's social, emotional and mental health needs have never been of more concern to teachers than they are now – this book genuinely brings theory to life and is essential reading for today's primary teachers, SENCOs, support staff and safeguarding leads.

Jean Gross has been a teacher, an educational psychologist, head of children's services in a local authority and a Visiting and Associate Fellow at three universities. She has written multiple books for Routledge, including *Time to Talk* (2018), *Reaching the Unseen Children* (2021) and *Beating Bureaucracy in Special Educational Needs* (2023).

Sarah Seleznyov is Co-Headteacher of School 360 and Strategic Lead for Learning and Development at Big Education Trust. She formerly worked at UCL Institute of Education and is the author of numerous articles and chapters on research approaches to teacher professional development.

T0373491

Improving Behaviour and Wellbeing in Primary Schools

Harnessing Social and Emotional Learning in the Classroom and Beyond

Edited by
Jean Gross and Sarah Seleznyov

Routledge
Taylor & Francis Group

LONDON AND NEW YORK

Designed cover image: © Getty Images

First published 2024
by Routledge
4 Park Square, Milton Park, Abingdon, Oxon OX14 4RN

and by Routledge
605 Third Avenue, New York, NY 10158

Routledge is an imprint of the Taylor & Francis Group, an informa business

British Library Cataloguing-in-Publication Data
A catalogue record for this book is available from the British Library

Library of Congress Cataloging-in-Publication Data
Names: Gross, Jean, editor. | Seleznyov, Sarah, editor.
Title: Improving behaviour and wellbeing in primary schools : harnessing social and emotional learning in the classroom and beyond / edited by Jean Gross and Sarah Seleznyov.
Description: Abingdon, Oxon ; New York, NY : Routledge, 2024. | Includes bibliographical references and index.
Identifiers: LCCN 2023037838 (print) | LCCN 2023037839 (ebook) | ISBN 9781032500737 (hardback) | ISBN 9781003396796 (paperback) | ISBN 9781003396796 (ebook)
Subjects: LCSH: Affective education—Great Britain—Case studies. | Social learning—Great Britain—Case studies. | Classroom environment—Great Britain—Case studies. | Child psychology—Great Britain—Case studies. | Education, Primary—Great Britain—Case studies.
Classification: LCC LB1072 .I664 2024 (print) | LCC LB1072 (ebook) | DDC 370.15/340941—dc23/eng/20231115
LC record available at https://lccn.loc.gov/2023037838
LC ebook record available at https://lccn.loc.gov/2023037839

ISBN: 978-1-032-50073-7 (hbk)
ISBN: 978-1-032-50072-0 (pbk)
ISBN: 978-1-003-39679-6 (ebk)

DOI: 10.4324/9781003396796

Typeset in Univers
by Apex CoVantage, LLC

Access the Support Material: www.routledge.com/9781032500720

Contents

About the editors

Jean Gross has been a teacher, an educational psychologist, head of children's services in a local authority, and a Visiting and Associate Fellow at three universities. She was formerly the government's Communication Champion for children. She was awarded a CBE for services to education in 2011 and has written multiple books for Routledge, including *Time to Talk* (2018), *Reaching the Unseen Children* (2021) and *Beating Bureaucracy in Special Educational Needs* (2023).

Sarah Seleznyov is Co-Headteacher of School 360, a primary school in London with a strong focus on social and emotional learning and wellbeing. She is also Strategic Lead for Learning and Development at Big Education Trust, an organisation seeking to support schools to approach education with a balance of Head, Heart and Hand. Sarah is also a PhD student at Vrije Universiteit Amsterdam and a published author.

Contributors

Aaron Bennett is a Year 5 teacher at Shaftesbury Primary School in Newham.

Stephen Goggin is a Year 5 teacher at Carpenter's Primary School in Newham.

Annabel Greyling is Inclusion Leader and Designated Safeguarding Lead at New City Primary School in Newham.

Melissa Hobbs is Assistant Headteacher at Carpenter's Primary School in Newham.

Lauren James was formerly a Reception teacher at School 21 in Newham.

Zainab Khonat is a Year 6 teacher at Shaftesbury Primary School in Newham.

Eilidh Kirkpatrick is a Year 4 teacher at New City Primary School in Newham.

Sarah Marriott is Headteacher at Pinner Wood Primary School in Harrow.

Maia Mitchell is Assistant Headteacher for Inclusion at Redriff Primary School in Southwark.

Una Murtagh is Assistant Headteacher and SENDCo at Drew Primary School in Newham.

Joanne O'Connor is Senior Deputy Headteacher at Shaftesbury Primary School in Newham.

Saidat Olajide is a Year 5 teacher at Portway Primary in Newham.

Laura Partington is a Year 3 teacher at Selwyn Primary School in Newham.

Lisa Placks is Assistant Headteacher at School 21 in Newham.

Susan Potter is Assistant Headteacher at Selwyn Primary School in Newham.

Casey Rich is Teaching and Learning Director and SENDCO at Portway Primary in Newham.

Jessica Robinson is a Year 6 teacher at Cubitt Town Primary School in Tower Hamlets.

Claire Taylor was formerly a Year 4 teacher at Redriff Primary School in Southwark.

Emily Thomas is a Lower Key Stage 2 Leader at Pinner Wood Primary School in Harrow.

Emma Whitwam is a Year 6 teacher and Year Group Leader at Cubitt Town Primary School in Tower Hamlets.

Demi Zoghby was formerly a Year 4 teacher at Drew Primary School in Newham.

Acknowledgements

The work described in this book was funded by The Laurel Trust, a charity that supports schools serving disadvantaged communities to make sustainable differences to children's learning and life chances. We are very grateful for the grant they provided and for all the support the Trust offered us throughout the lifetime of the project.

Many of the schools involved in the project drew on the work of Leah Kuypers, who created the Zones of Regulation curriculum framework, a systematic, cognitive-behavioural approach used to teach children how to regulate their feelings, energy and sensory needs. We are very grateful to Leah for her inspiration.

We would also like to thank Dr John Ivens from The Bethlem and Maudsley Hospital School for his support with the project.

1 What works in improving behaviour and wellbeing

Jean Gross

This book is about the work of a group of primary teachers and leaders, who together set out to make a difference in the behaviour and wellbeing of the children in their school. The next chapter describes the project they took part in; subsequent chapters are written by the teachers themselves.

I had the privilege of contributing a theoretical framework to their work to help the teachers choose a direction for their own classroom-based research. This chapter explains the ideas we explored.

A perspective on behaviour

Every teacher worries about children's behaviour. There is no shortage of guidance on how to manage behaviour in the classroom: how to set rules, develop routines, use praise and sanctions. Most of this is very useful. Yet it tends to be based on a rather limited model – one that says that children know how to behave and will do so if we get the classroom conditions right.

This may be true for some children, but not all. Dealing with 'behaviour difficulties' can be likened to dealing with reading difficulties, spelling difficulties, difficulties in learning maths. If children can't read, spell or do computations, we teach them. We would not dream of punishing them if they could not read a word; nor would we see rewards (other than the satisfaction of learning something new) as appropriate for English or maths.

So it should be for behaviour. If children don't behave, it may be that we need to actively teach them the skills that underpin positive behaviour. Skills like managing their feelings, getting on with others, resolving conflict and handling frustration and failure.

> When children don't know how to read, we teach.
> When children don't know how to write, we teach.
> But if a child doesn't know how to behave, we … teach? … punish?
> Why can't we finish the last sentence as automatically as we do the others?

(**Tom Herner**, former president of the National Association of Special Educators (quoted in Allen, **2020**))

DOI: 10.4324/9781003396796-1

This was the premise that informed the work of the teachers we celebrate in this book. Each of them found ways to develop children's social and emotional skills in their classes. They researched strategies, tried them out and evaluated the impact. And the results were outstanding.

Why don't children behave?

I like to think of children with behavioural difficulties as falling into four (often overlapping) categories (Figure 1.1). The model I've developed helps, I think, to understand why, in the words of Lori Desautels (2019): 'traditional discipline works best with the children who need it the least, and works least with the children who need it the most.'

Children who can behave but choose not to

Some children and young people – those in the top circle in the diagram – *can* behave appropriately, but don't choose to. They have the social and emotional skills that underlie positive behaviour. They can get on with others, manage their feelings and motivate themselves when they want to. They choose not to apply these skills, however, because the rewards for not doing so (like making classmates laugh, or not having to finish a hard piece of work if they are sent out of a lesson) outweigh those for behaving well. Short suspensions may not bother them because they can spend time at home gaming and watching YouTube.

These children can relatively easily change their behaviour if we take time to find out what sanctions would actually act as a deterrent, and which rewards would motivate them.

Constant 'tellings-off' are unlikely to be successful. One study (Reinke, Herman and Newcomer, 2016) observed primary teachers' interactions with pupils at the start of the school year, and then followed the pupils up

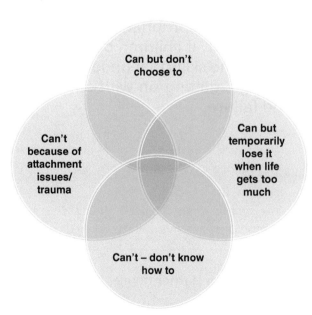

Figure 1.1   Four reasons why children might not behave

later. Children who initially received mainly negative feedback were rated at the end of the year as having a significant increase in behaviour problems, whereas children who received more positive feedback demonstrated significant increases in positive behaviours.

Increasing the amount of praise given for positive behaviour has consistently been found to be effective. Studies in which the ratio of praise to reprimands was deliberately increased in classrooms show that the higher the teacher's praise-to-reprimand ratio was, the higher the children's levels of on-task behaviour (Caldarella et al., 2020).

So for children who 'can but choose not to', we can focus on positive behaviour and tactically ignore minor misbehaviours. We can use the kind of assertive but polite language that tells children what behaviour is expected rather than what we don't want them to be doing – 'The behaviour I want to see right now is ...., thank you.' We should always comment on the behaviour, not the pupil: 'That was unkind behaviour and not how we talk to each other in our class', rather than 'You're unkind and unhelpful.'

The children who can behave but temporarily lose it when life gets too much

Some children do not lack the social and emotional skills they need in order to behave well, but may not be able to maintain them because they are under stress. They might be caring for a sick or disabled parent, perhaps; they might be witnessing domestic violence, or have experienced a recent bereavement.

Action may need to be taken, of course, to try and sort out the family stressors or events that are troubling them. But these children can also be helped by school systems that recognise when they are under stress.

Examples might be systems like regular emotional check-ins for all at the start of the day, and perhaps after the lunch break, as a way of noticing any child who might be feeling angry, sad or anxious – as well as of helping children learn to be aware of and express their own emotions rather than act them out in unhelpful ways.

This was an approach taken by many of the schools contributing chapters to this book.

Ideally, the school will have established recognised spaces to which pupils can take themselves voluntarily and for a limited time if they need to calm down – a special room, or a corner of a primary classroom equipped with things like smooth pebbles to handle, intricate patterns to colour in, a lava lamp, lavender-scented cotton balls and a rocking chair.

Another idea for these children is the 'ten per cent kinder' strategy, where those who are having a difficult time at home are highlighted to all staff, who simply make a point of going out of their way to show interest and warmth whenever they see them.

Children who can't behave because of attachment difficulties/trauma

This group of children tax our behaviour systems the most. They have a short fuse and swing between moods in ways that are hard to understand. They may have great difficulties forming any sort of relationship, with adults and peers. Many will never have felt loved or learned to regulate emotions through early interaction with a warm, responsive adult. They may also have experienced significant trauma, so their nervous systems are in permanent trip-wire state; they don't feel safe so we need to help them feel safe in school, and get them some specialist help.

Often we think of trauma as a dramatic event like an earthquake, terrorism or an assault. A broader definition encompasses any event or series of events that overwhelms a person's capacity to cope and has a long-lasting impact on them. All too many of the children we teach have experienced trauma of this kind.

To help them feel safe, it is important to build a strong bond of trust with at least one person in school, and if that adult is not in school there should be another key adult the pupil knows well, to whom they can turn when they are upset. These children need 'safe faces' as well as the calming places (safe spaces) we have already touched on.

It is also helpful if their class teachers take active steps to build the relationship with the child – even though this may be difficult. These children may push adults away, and actively provoke rejection, because that is what they are used to. They will also test any adult they are beginning to trust, by behaving in ever more challenging ways in order to find out whether that adult will still care about them. In the words of a popular quote, attributed to Dr Russell Barkley: 'The children who need love the most will always ask for it in the most unloving ways.'

Tips for building the relationship

- Take extra care to greet the child first thing, every day, and have a quick 'problem-free' chat about something they are interested in.
- Try having lunch with them from time to time.
- Involve them in any lunchtime or after school club you run.
- Try to listen to them without giving advice or opinions, acknowledging their feelings (I can see you're really upset', 'That must have made you very angry/frustrated … ').
- Don't be afraid to show the child you care about them: 'You are very important to me and I really want you to do well at school.'

It can help these children if we create a personalised workspace somewhere in the school which has their name, a picture of things they like, a go-to box of things that calm them down (a photo, feather for breathing, a smooth stone to touch, a calming bottle of glitter that slowly settles after you shake it) and their personal school timetable on display. For some children, we might provide alternatives to the playground, perhaps via lunchtime clubs, so as to avoid placing them in social situations they are not for the moment able to navigate.

Children with attachment difficulties or trauma can, to an extent, benefit from classroom strategies to develop their social and emotional skills, such as regulating strong emotions. They can certainly benefit from being a part of a class where other children have well-developed social and emotional capabilities, so that they are able to show empathy towards troubled peers and help them to cope. But they will also need intensive and specialist help.

For this reason we did not recommend that the teachers involved in the work described in this book base their research on children with difficulties like these – simply because they were unlikely to be able to show a measurable impact within the project's timeframe. Some of them did target these children, however, and some saw very good outcomes, as you will find out later.

Children who can't behave because they don't know how to

Ordinary behaviour management strategies also may not work for another group of children – those in the bottom circle of my behaviour model diagram, who don't have in their repertoire the social and emotional capabilities they need in order to behave well. Providing more rewards or adjusting the type of sanction won't work if they don't, for example, know how to recognise and manage their feelings. They won't work if they don't know how to handle frustration or control their anger. They won't work if they lack the social skills needed for working in groups.

As we have seen, you can't punish (or reward) a child into doing something they don't know how to do. These children need the kind of help that the teachers involved in this book succeeded in providing.

What are social and emotional skills, and what is the impact if we teach them?

The definition of social and emotional learning on which the teachers' work celebrated in this book was based is that of the Education Endowment Foundation (Van Poortvliet, Clarke and Gross, 2019). In turn, that definition comes from the US-based Collaborative for Academic, Social and Emotional Learning (CASEL), which describes it as:

> The process through which all young people and adults acquire and apply the knowledge, skills, and attitudes to develop healthy identities, manage emotions and achieve personal and collective goals, feel and show empathy for others, establish and maintain supportive relationships, and make responsible and caring decisions.
>
> (CASEL, 2020)

CASEL groups social and emotional skills into five categories (Figure 1.2).

- Self-awareness: To know and understand oneself and one's emotions.
- Self-management: To regulate, manage and motivate one's actions and emotions.
- Social awareness: To understand those around us and show empathy.

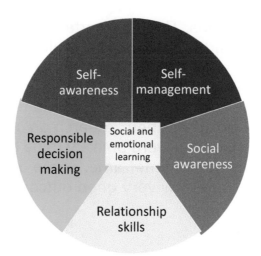

Figure 1.2   Social and emotional learning

- Relationship skills: To interact with others in a positive and effective way.
- Responsible decision-making: To make decisions and take actions as a member of society with rights and responsibilities.

We know from a large body of research that developing these five skills or capabilities in schools leads to improved behaviour, mental health and attainment (Van Poortvliet, Clarke and Gross, 2019). A recent study, for example (Durlak, Mahoney and Boyle, in press), reviewed 12 meta-analyses of universal, school-based social and emotional learning (SEL) programmes for children from early childhood education through secondary school, involving an estimated one million students. It found consistent, positive impacts on a broad range of student outcomes including self-esteem and self-efficacy, school bonding (positive attitudes towards school), prosocial behaviours (like helping others), levels of emotional distress and frequency of 'conduct problems.'

Academic achievement also improved. One study, for example, which reviewed the outcomes of over 200 evidence-based curricular programmes that aimed to develop social and emotional skills found that when properly implemented they generate an 11 percentage point uplift to average attainment scores (Durlak et al., 2011). These are large gains, larger than those achieved by most school improvement initiatives. Given these findings, it is surprising that social and emotional learning is not embedded in every school's curriculum.

In many cases, the effects of SEL programmes are long-lasting. One meta-analysis (Taylor et al., 2017) looked at several school-based SEL studies that had follow-ups six months or longer after the initial intervention and found sustained effects on positive attitudes towards self, others and school; academic performance; emotional distress; and risky behaviours. The effects on wellbeing were evident up to 18 years later.

All these findings only applied, however, when the SEL programme that was used had certain qualities, which CASEL and the EEF (Education Endowment Foundation) describe using the acronym SAFE (Sequenced, Active, Focused, Explicit).

The SAFE acronym

Sequenced: there is a proper curriculum progression in the skills taught, with learning in one age group or lesson building on what the children had learned in earlier classes.

Active: children learn through active techniques like role play and discussion rather than just 'teaching from the front.'

Focused: children learn in short but regular sessions built into the timetable.

Explicit: teachers are clear about which particular SEL capabilities they are seeking to develop in any one lesson.

How are social and emotional skills developed?

Social and emotional skills can be developed in schools through the curriculum, through everyday classroom teaching and learning and through the school and classroom environment.

They can be *woven into subject lessons*. Empathy, for example, can be developed in English lessons in which a pupil adopts the role of one of the characters in a novel and, sitting in a 'hotseat', is asked questions about what they are thinking and feeling. In geography, pupils might learn about early explorers and identify the motivations and qualities that drove them to overcome overwhelming odds. The ability to see multiple perspectives (necessary for empathy) can be developed in history when we examine conflicts and what led up to them.

Social and emotional skills can also be developed through *classroom routines*, such as starting the day with a 'check-in' activity or using tools to help children recognise that they need to regulate strong feelings whenever a behaviour issue is on the horizon. Many of the teachers who describe their work in the chapters that follow drew on routines like these in their research.

The *classroom and school environment* presents another opportunity to develop the skills that underpin positive behaviour. There might, for example, be displays: visuals of taught calming exercises, an emotion check-in board, a worry box where children can post a message about what is worrying them and a similar private 'I wish my teacher knew … ' box. There might be an empathy or conflict resolution corner, perhaps with pairs of cut-out footprints so children can try standing in someone else's shoes and saying how they might be thinking and feeling. 'Friendship stops' in the playground might be set up to encourage children to notice anyone standing alone and sweep them up into their games. Within the classroom or in a central part of the school there might be an area where children can go when they need to calm down.

These environmental adaptations also formed part of the work described in this book.

Finally, social and emotional skills can be developed through the school's *PSHE/RSE curriculum*, with carefully designed lessons. This too happened in our research schools. To be effective, such lessons require a planned and age-related progression in the specific skills to be taught. Just as we have a planned progression in learning objectives for reading or maths, so that the skills we are developing in Year 6 build on but do not duplicate the skills children have learned in Year 1, or 3, or 5. The SEL curriculum also requires dedicated time if it is to be effective – the EEF recommend 30–60 minutes of teaching per week.

Taught or caught?

> Interventions are most effective when they use a 'taught' (skills instruction) and 'caught' (classroom and whole-school climate) approach. A whole-school approach defines the entire school community as the unit of change and involves coordinated action between three interrelated components: (i) curriculum, teaching, and learning; (ii) school ethos and environment; (iii) family and community partnerships.

(M. Gedikoglu, 2021)

Education expert David Hargreaves once described two components of the school curriculum – the 'taught' and the 'caught.' The taught curriculum is the overt subject matter; the caught is the implicit learning which pupils absorb from the school environment and the behaviours unconsciously modelled by adults.

As we have seen, the evidence shows that social and emotional learning requires a 'taught' element. It should have a place in a carefully sequenced, regularly taught curriculum. Nevertheless, it also needs to be 'caught.' Children need the adults in school to model social and emotional skills, from showing empathy to relating well to others to identifying their feelings ('Oh no my laptop's frozen … I'm feeling really frustrated and cross') and moving productively through them ('I need to do my calm breathing for a bit … OK that's better').

Children also need opportunities to deploy and develop the skills they have begun to acquire in discrete teaching sessions across the school day. They might practise conflict resolution in the playground, for example, or older pupils might develop social awareness by taking a defined role in buddying younger ones. Children might be involved in restorative justice practices, through which they learn to see others' perspectives, confront the consequences of their actions and repair relationships. In the classroom, they might be asked to set themselves their own stretching goals and learn how to break them down into small steps and find ways to cope with setbacks.

The school's behaviour policy, too, will need to align with the idea of teaching children the social and emotional skills they need in order to behave well. It will need to recognise, for example, that being able to talk about feelings underpins positive behaviour choices in emotionally charged situations. It will need to acknowledge that poor behaviour is often the result of unsuccessful emotion regulation, and that emotion regulation also needs to be taught and practised. Whatever way the school chooses to celebrate or reward 'good behaviour' (praise in assemblies, notes to parents and carers, peer nominations) will need to be adapted so that instead it is used to celebrate children and adults who have demonstrated particular social and emotional skills.

Parental involvement will need to be considered. Family workshops might be introduced to help parents and carers understand the school's policy and share their child's learning. At these workshops, parents and carers can explore ways they can model and scaffold the skills that are being taught in school.

Social and emotional learning, then, needs a whole-school approach where it is 'caught' as well as 'taught.' From the start, the teachers involved in the project described in this book planned ways in which the ideas they were piloting in their own classrooms could be embedded in wider school practices.

Is social and emotional learning relevant to all children?

The schools that are the focus of this book often evaluated the success of their work by looking at the impact on particular children with social, emotional or mental health needs (SEMH). Nevertheless, most of the teachers involved made their projects 'universal': that is, they introduced approaches they could use with their whole class. That, after all, is what busy teachers need to do. They do not often have time for targeted work with individuals or groups.

There is, in fact, good evidence that making SEL 'universal' benefits all children, not just a few. When I look back on my own education, for example, I know that I personally would have benefited from the opportunities provided in SEL curricula to learn to be better at bouncing back after failure, lifting a negative mood, managing worries and avoiding uncontrolled angry outbursts.

As a parent I wanted, too, for my own children to have the chance, in the particular social context that a school provides, to learn about peer pressure and to practise the assertiveness skills that would enable them to withstand risky behaviours in adolescence. I wanted school, home and community to align in a shared effort to help my children learn how to communicate their feelings, set themselves goals and work towards them, interact successfully with others, resolve conflicts peaceably, cope with stress and negotiate their way through the many complex relationships in their lives, today and tomorrow.

As a psychologist, I have always believed that our own internal environment, the way our brains work (or sometimes fail to work effectively when flooded with adrenaline and cortisol), should be as much a legitimate subject of study as the physical environment we inhabit. In my view, we should spend time learning to understand ourselves and our emotions, as well as acquiring knowledge about literature, science, mathematics, geography and history.

Even in the best-kept emotional landscapes of home and community, opportunities to acquire empathy, grit and responsibility are in decline. What were once intergenerational communities framed around the village shop or church or extended family have increasingly been replaced by the single-generation social networks of a social media generation. Once, when interacting with people much older, or very different from themselves, young people learned about perspective-taking and empathy. Once, when observing or helping with the care of much younger family members, they learned about emotional regulation and responsibility. These days have passed and will not return. Schools, therefore, have a part to play in making up for the opportunities lost as a result of social change.

As with any learning, some children need more help with social and emotional learning than others. But universal SEL programmes lay the groundwork for any extra help some children may need. Universal teaching means that any 'extra' is not a bolt-on activity, undertaken out of class with a teaching assistant (TA) or learning mentor and detached from learning in class. Just as with reading or maths interventions, what children do out of class needs to be connected with what they have already worked on in class. Class teacher, child and TA or learning mentor need a shared vocabulary and shared learning objectives. Any extra help children have will then make sense to them, and enable the 'extra' to be backed up by the class teacher throughout the day and week.

There are three further reasons why working on SEL with the whole class is an essential backdrop to interventions with children with SEMH.

- It allows for three levels of 'waves' of intervention (Figure 1.3), where the better the provision at the base of the triangle, the fewer children will actually need targeted help.
- It helps create the kind of classroom environments where children with social, emotional and behavioural difficulties will be supported by their peers – because classmates will have developed their own skills of empathy, being a good friend, handling conflict and being resilient in the face of difficulties.

Figure 1.3   Waves of intervention

● It allows for the whole-school systems and environments which give pupils the chance to apply the learning from any extra, targeted help they may receive.

The science of emotion regulation

Social and emotional learning is, as we have seen, about developing capabilities or skills in five different areas. Many of the teachers who contributed to this book chose to focus their work primarily on one of these areas – self-management or self-regulation. They became interested in the neuroscience behind self-regulation, and in some cases developed lessons to teach children some of this neuroscience too.

In simple terms, neuroscience teaches us that the human brain is made up of three main components:

● The neocortex, where thinking, imagining and planning take place. We use this part of the brain to think critically, solve problems and make decisions. In evolutionary terms, it is the 'newest' part of the brain to develop, and particularly well developed in humans.
● The limbic system, which looks after emotion processing and memory. This is said to be the second oldest brain structure. It is sometimes called 'the mammalian brain' because it is present in all mammals.
● The brain stem and cerebellum, which looks after physiological functions that are outside of our conscious control, such as reflexes, breathing, heart rate and digestion. It was the earliest part of the brain to evolve and is sometimes called the 'reptilian brain.'

Children often enjoy a simplified model of these components which talks about the 'upstairs brain' (the neocortex) and the 'downstairs brain' (the limbic system and brain stem). The upstairs brain, we can tell them, allows us to think before we act. It helps us make sensible choices and manage our learning.

The 'downstairs brain', in contrast, looks after the basic things that help us survive. It developed at a time when life was dangerous for humans, who had to be ready at all times to react quickly to threats, from wild animals to aggressors from other tribes. So this part of the brain enables us to act fast, without taking time to think and weigh up options. It looks after what is called the 'fight or flight response' when we experience acute fear and our whole body gets ready to either run away from the threat or fight back.

In the fight or flight response, our heart will beat faster, and we breathe faster and more shallowly, so as to get more oxygen. Our stomach may churn, because digestion stops so as to direct all energy and blood flow to the muscles. Our hands and feet may tingle because the blood flow has been redirected to the large muscles. Our throat and chest may feel tight because our body is tensing ready to flee or attack.

When we are in fight or flight mode, our limbic system overrides the neocortex. We go into emotional overdrive. And while this worked well to protect us in caveman times, it often isn't appropriate to the way we live today. Life is much less dangerous, but our evolution hasn't yet caught up with that fact. We are, essentially, still cavepeople – but with the internet.

Our brains have evolved for survival, rather than for emotional wellbeing (our own or that of others). Nowadays, our feelings can build up and we can end up losing control just as a result of the accumulating frustrations of everyday life – which, for children in school, includes everyday classrooms and playgrounds.

This happens to all of us. It happens particularly often for those who have experienced trauma or chronic stress, which can result in a brain that is 'stuck' in a state of high alert, primed to activate fight or flight responses at any time.

The way to regulate emotions

We can, in schools, help children learn how to recognise that they are nearing the point where emotions might hi-jack their thinking brain, and take action if necessary to control otherwise overwhelming feelings like anger or anxiety.

There are many different strategies children can use to self-regulate, which the teachers contributing to this book describe in the chapters that follow. One of these is deep, relaxed breathing. This works because it 'tricks' the brain into believing that all is well. If we are breathing slowly and calmly, our heart rate will slow and our muscles relax; feedback from our bodies convinces the 'upstairs brain' that there is now no danger.

When we calm ourselves through breathing or other strategies, we are 'down-regulating', moving from a state of high alertness and intense emotions to a place of calm. Sometimes, however, we need to 'up-regulate.' When we feel sluggish or 'down', we might engage in some high-intensity physical activity or listen to upbeat music so as to increase our alertness and ability to engage with the outside world.

Many of the teachers involved in the project described in this book used a particular approach to self-regulation that includes 'up-regulation' as well as the more familiar 'down-regulation.' The approach, originally devised to support autistic children, is called Zones of Regulation (Kuypers, 2021), and has proved useful to a much wider group.

The Zones approach involves children in identifying which of four 'Zones' they are in at any given moment:

The Blue Zone, in which we are in a low state of alertness and may be feeling sad, tired or bored.

The Green Zone, in which we are calm but alert and may be feeling focused and happy or content.

The Yellow Zone, in which our emotions are heightened but we are still in control. We may be excited, fidgety, anxious, nervous or act 'silly.'

The Red Zone, in which our emotions have tipped over so that in one way or another we have 'lost it.' We may experience terror, panic or rage, or feel devastated.

All of the Zones are natural experiences, and all have their place. What is inappropriate in one context may be perfectly appropriate in another; when playing an exciting game outside in the playground on a windy day, there might, for example, be no need for children to get out of the Yellow Zone. Sometimes staying in the Blue Zone gives us time to rest before we re-energise, or turn inward to work through a problem we need to solve. When we face an immediate threat, we might need to be in the Red Zone to help us escape the danger. Children should be taught that all emotions are OK (even anger); it is what we do with them – the behaviours they lead to – that may not be OK.

The idea, however, is that if children have identified themselves as being in the Yellow Zone inappropriately, they will proactively use strategies to pull themselves back from the edge of losing control; if they are in the Blue Zone they can choose to increase their state of alertness and positive mood.

It is not difficult to see how effective self-regulation using the Zones can help with behaviour and mental health problems – stopping children from getting into arguments or fights, reducing anxiety so they can cope with potentially stressful events and tackling low mood that can lead to depression. Equally, however, self-regulation is about improving children's ability to *learn*. There is a quote from Dr Bruce Perry that explains this perfectly:

The brain is made up of a series of complex systems, only one of which (the top part of the brain) is responsible for thinking. These systems are related to and dependent on each other. If a child is emotionally unregulated (upset, distracted, fidgety, or bored) and doesn't have self-regulation skills and strategies, learning is that much more difficult and inefficient.

The best way to make the top part of the brain receptive to learning is to make sure these lower parts of the brain are regulated.

(Dr Bruce Perry, 2009)

Back to behaviour, wellbeing – and learning

As this chapter has made clear, focusing on developing social and emotional skills has proved itself an effective way of improving wellbeing and behaviour. It is an approach that can be used with whole classes, as well as with children with identified social, emotional and mental health needs. What has also been made clear is that the approach is fundamental to improving learning and achievement.

So far we have looked at theory. What is needed to back up the theory, however, are examples of what a social and emotional learning approach looks like in real classrooms, in real playgrounds and in real schools. It is this that you will find in the chapters that follow.

Key takeaways

- If children don't behave well, they may need to be taught the social and emotional skills that underpin positive behaviour and wellbeing.
- Social and emotional skills include self-awareness, self-management, social awareness, relationship skills and responsible decision-making.
- There is good evidence that programmes which explicitly develop these social and emotional skills lead to long-term improvements in behaviour and learning.
- Social and emotional skills can be developed in school through the curriculum, through everyday classroom teaching and learning and through the environment.
- Working on social and emotional skills with a whole class benefits all children, and helps ensure a supportive classroom context for children who struggle most with behaviour or wellbeing.
- Identifying how they are feeling and having an understanding of basic neuroscience can help children learn how to regulate their emotions.

2 The action research project

Sarah Seleznyov

This chapter describes how the action research project worked: how the project was designed to help participating schools bring about change, how the schools each framed a research question and how they evaluated their chosen approach.

The context

The last few years have taught us a lot about the importance of considering children's mental health and wellbeing. The COVID years and particularly the impact of the lockdowns on the mental health of children and young people only served to reinforce the belief that wellbeing is crucial for learning as well as life, and that wellbeing can be improved through the actions of school leaders and teachers.

As the Headteacher of School 360, a brand new school in Newham, London, I was aware that the impact of lockdowns on our first cohort of Reception children had been acute. I was interested in undertaking work with local schools to find ways of addressing mental health and wellbeing issues.

My own school is part of a Trust (The Big Education Trust) which has a particular commitment to educating the 'whole child.' Our curriculum model across the Trust is one of Head (academic learning), Heart (wellbeing and relationships) and Hand (skills and creativity) in equal measure. All Big Education schools seek to support the wellbeing of pupils, parents and staff as a crucial aspect of school success.

Newham is an area serving families experiencing multiple deprivation and challenges: 22% of pupils in Newham schools come from low-income families, with over 38% receiving Free School Meals (well above the London average of 28% and England average of 22%). Social, Emotional and Mental Health (SEMH) need is one of the Newham's High Need categories and these pupils represent over 17% of those receiving SEND support. National data showed that COVID was likely to have exacerbated this need, due to the social isolation and emotional distress caused by lockdowns. We also knew that pupils living in poverty were more likely to exhibit SEMH needs, meaning this was a particular priority for local schools.

As the number of pupils with a diagnosis of SEMH had increased over recent years, school budgets had shrunk, and schools' access to external expertise and the numbers of support staff they could deploy to support

DOI: 10.4324/9781003396796-2

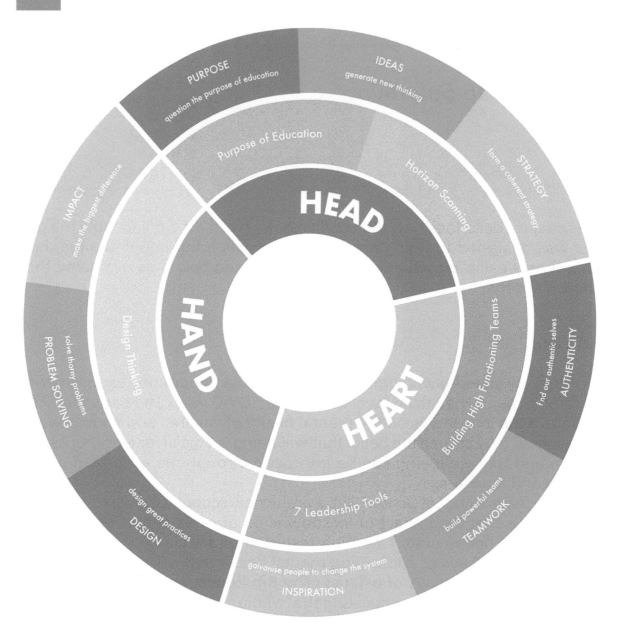

Figure 2.1 Big Education's Head, Heart, Hand model

such pupils had decreased. These budget challenges have left us seeking cost-effective solutions to meeting the emotional and wellbeing needs of pupils in all our schools.

Thanks to generous funding from The Laurel Trust, we were able to fund a research project for 11 schools in London to improve the learning experience for pupils with SEMH concerns. We had a firm belief that interventions to improve wellbeing and mental health for SEMH pupils would be likely to have a positive impact on the learning and wellbeing of all pupils, as they emerged from the COVID pandemic. The project would enable participating schools to design changes to practice based on recent evidence on mental health and wellbeing, to trial these changes, to measure their impact and to share their findings with colleagues in their own schools, with other schools on the project and schools beyond this.

The funding from The Laurel Trust enabled us to access expert support from Jean Gross, leading author and national expert on SEMH and one of the authors of this book, and also from Dr John Ivens, an experienced psychologist and Headteacher of The Bethlem and Maudsley Hospital School for children with mental illness.

The design of the research project

The design of the project was one which intended to enable teacher agency. Godfrey (2017) distinguishes between three approaches to research for teachers:

- 'evidence-based practice', a passive process in which teaching approaches are based on evidence about 'what works' produced by academics;
- 'evidence-informed practice', whereby teachers actively combine evidence from academic research, practitioner enquiry (for example, lesson study or action research) and other school-level data;
- 'research-informed practice', whereby teachers engage in and with academic and practitioner forms of research, using evidence from both to make changes to practices.

This project focused specifically on the third, 'research-informed practice', since it supported teachers to use research evidence within practitioner action research to make a difference in their own context and for their own pupils. The project drew heavily on the Research Learning Communities model developed by Brown (2017) and did not involve the passive receipt of research and an evaluation of implementation and impact, but a project that combined both research and teacher expertise to find out what worked for their pupils, their classes and their schools.

Schools were encouraged to send both a senior leader and a class teacher to a series of workshops across a year, and in these workshops, they worked through a cycle of inquiry collaboratively. The role of the senior leader was to enable the class teacher to access resources, such as time out of class or use of whole-school professional development time, as well as to enable changes to whole-school policy and practice. The teacher could test the intervention they designed, tweak and improve it, and then champion it with colleagues, telling stories of impact on pupils and sharing strategies for implementation.

We knew that teachers often find research tricky to access and understand, so asked Jean Gross to collate a set of accessible readings for participants and to start the first workshop with a presentation and question-and-answer session on what we know about the best ways to improve learning and well-being for pupils with SEMH needs.

Based on this presentation, participants were then encouraged to go away and read further and deeper from the set of readings, following lines of enquiry from the literature that felt most relevant to them in their context. There were several themes from the literature that schools were particularly interested in: recent increases in anxiety and emotional issues since the COVID pandemic; how to understand the root causes of outwardly negative pupil behaviours including issues such as low self-worth and dysregulation;

the need to consider pupils having different capacities to manage their own emotions and that these may fluctuate over time; the positive impact of teaching social and emotional skills to pupils; and the need for adults themselves to build emotional literacy and strategies to self-regulate.

Gathering baseline data and framing research questions

Once teachers had explored the literature and thought about how it related to pupils they knew, they were encouraged to gather some baseline data on these pupils, so that they could be sure they had a deep understanding of the challenges as understood by a variety of stakeholders.

We helped teachers explore a range of tools for gathering data, such as the Leuven Scale (https://emotionallyhealthyschools.org/primary/the-leuven-scale/), and a set of tools designed by Dr John Ivens, including a school wellbeing survey for pupils aged seven and over, and a Happiness Line for wellbeing conversations with younger pupils. We then helped teachers design their own tools so that the data they collected was specific to the problem they had identified. We helped them understand how to design survey, interview and observation tools that could provide useful data, and to consider what sets of pre-existing school data might shed light on their pupils, for example behaviour tracking or assessment data. The principle was one of triangulation, using a variety of data sources, both qualitative and quantitative, to understand the challenge and design the intervention, as well as to eventually measure its impact.

Once teachers had explored the literature and analysed their data, we helped them construct a research question, using a technique that helps people work collaboratively on question design. Each school team presented their challenge, focus and perspective on what they wanted to achieve, to a group of colleagues from other schools (Figure 2.2). Each member of the group then took a pad of Post-it notes and, very quickly, without thinking too hard, used the sentence stems below to generate as many possible research questions as they could:

- How can we …?
- Under what conditions …?
- What is the best way to …?
- Will … make a difference to …?
- What strategies …?
- What can we do to … so that …?

Once a huge pile of questions had been generated, the school team laid them out, looked for patterns in terms of keywords or phrases and for wording that resonated with what they knew about their pupils and what they wanted to achieve. They then used these identified words and phrases to construct a final research question.

This process tried to mitigate against the tendency to think really hard about a research question and to try to get the wording absolutely right on

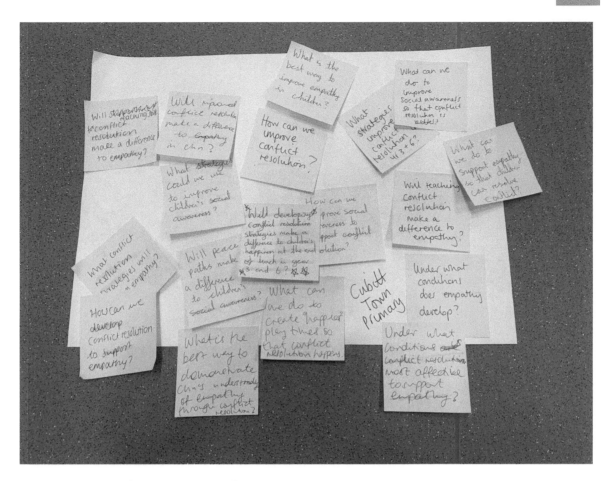

Figure 2.2   Deciding on a research question

the first attempt. By freeing up the brain to explore many possible questions, school teams are able to explore different options and narrow down their thinking with the support of colleagues as critical friends.

Participants then used an innovative technique to build a physical model of the situation they wanted to change. Using Lego, craft materials and paper, they created a 3D model of the problem as they saw it, and everything and everyone involved in that problem. This approach (Brown, 2017) helped the school teams to develop a deeper understanding of the situation through shared language or metaphor (Heracleous and Jacobs, 2008).

They explained their models to other schools on the project, who asked critical questions to help the school teams think deeply about these pupils and the possible solutions they might design. They were also able to take away photographs of the models to share with colleagues in their schools at a later date (Figure 2.3).

Next steps

The combined thinking resulting from the literature review, the baseline data analysis, the research question and the 3D modelling activity enabled schools to draw up plans for their intervention or change to practice, and its implementation.

Figure 2.3   3D model of the situation to be tackled

One of the important goals of the project was to enable school teams to influence whole-school policy and practice, designing an intervention that could be shared with and used by colleagues so that more pupils with SEMH needs could benefit. There were several simple resources provided to enable sharing, for example a poster template helped them present their proposed project to the school; a case study template enabled them to report on their project outcomes; and a PowerPoint template enabled them to present their findings and evidence of impact to colleagues. Input on enabling change was also taught, as well as its implementation in schools, for example learning about Adopter Types (Rogers, 2003) and using social network analysis (Otte and Rousseau, 2002), to identify patterns of informal influence within groups and possible 'champions' for the project in their schools.

Throughout the four face-to-face sessions, school teams were encouraged to act as critical friends to each other, explaining and justifying their analyses, decisions and plans, sharing successes and challenges and learning from each other's projects and experiences.

The project ended with a celebration event at which all schools presented the full scope of their project: research question, baseline and impact data, intervention and implementation details, challenges and successes, personal learning and future plans. This was a joyous occasion, at which participants experienced a sense of satisfaction about what they had achieved. It was also an opportunity for further learning: several wanted to learn more about each other's projects and try them out in their own schools.

Reflecting on the programme

Participating teachers felt that the programme had been 'worthwhile' and 'rewarding' and that they had gained 'deep insight' into the issue of SEMH. Assigning time to read around and reflect on practices before implementing them was seen as particularly useful. Several teachers said that they now had better strategies to regulate themselves and create a calmer classroom experience for pupils.

Furthermore, staff talked about a new recognition and understanding of pupils who respond differently to intense emotions, varying from suppression and anxiety to outbursts and anger. They also felt they were now better able to recognise and tackle the more complex needs of children who had experienced trauma, abuse or neglect, and were better equipped to know when more specialist support for those children would be needed:

> As a class teacher it is all too easy to get wrapped up in the curriculum and the pressure that entails without always taking time to consider the needs of each child in the class; whether they are being met on a deep enough level and how this may be resulting in a variety of behaviours in school and indeed at home. The time we have taken to not only think about this ourselves but also to include other members of staff and consider small changes that we can make and different perspectives we can view them from, has already begun to pay dividends. It is gratifying to be here at the start of what I am sure will be a long-term process.

(Teacher)

Participants also appreciated opportunities to understand and explore how influence can spread across the school, as a way of supporting implementation:

> I have learnt a lot about the importance of my role in supporting staff to make the changes necessary to support children's SEMH … New initiatives, changes to timetable – and the additional planning that this entails – can sometimes be a barrier to staff, who in schools are often already stretched. When our team could see research in action, having an observable impact on the children they teach/ work with each day, this was immediately motivating.

(Leader)

Schools felt the practices they had tested as part of the project were now embedded within school policy and practice so should have longevity.

The cross-school nature of the project enabled learning, through the cycles of planning, reflection and critical talk in the face-to-face sessions:

> *We have both gained a great deal from this project and have benefited from discussing, sharing and collaborating with other schools. The research and discussion and planning we undertook were something we enjoyed, and we frequently finished our sessions feeling invigorated and motivated to make this project a success.*

(Teacher)

Many schools felt that the programme was also positively impacting attitudes to research in schools in the following ways:

- research engagement being seen as a key tool for professional development;
- developing their skills to formulate more succinct research questions;
- a greater understanding of the need for future projects to be evidence-based;
- knowledge of the key steps or processes involved in running a research project for any future investigations.

All concluded that research-informed practices designed for pupils with specific SEMH needs can have a broader impact on the wellbeing and mental health of all pupils. The Zones of Regulation tool was one approach that worked well in multiple contexts and with various cohorts of pupils, and was relatively simple to implement as a whole-school practice.

In short, relatively simple changes to practices can make a huge difference to emotional wellbeing and mental health, and when implemented through an action research approach, there is a greater chance of successful implementation, as well as learning for successful future problem-solving and school change projects.

3 Conker the chameleon

How we taught children about the Zones of Regulation at Drew Primary School

Demi Zoghby and Una Murtagh

Our school is a two-form entry primary school, serving an area of high social deprivation.

We worked with two Year 4 classes, where a number of children were really struggling with their emotional regulation. These children were in the middle of Year 2 during the first COVID pandemic lockdown and missed a term of Year 3; this had affected their behaviour and wellbeing. They were therefore the ideal year group in which to introduce a programme of social and emotional learning.

The children

Within both Year 4 classes there was a group of children who we thought would particularly benefit from this input.

Child A has Social Communication difficulties and struggles to engage with learning. This was so acute that as a team we decided he would spend the mornings in a nurture group. A recent assessment by the Educational Psychologist confirmed that he is a child who would benefit from an ongoing emotion regulation programme.

Child B is a middle child of seven children; the youngest is only six months old. We assumed that his family situation meant he found the demands of the classroom overwhelming because there were so many expectations on him to look after his younger siblings at home. Recent assessments by our Educational Psychologist revealed, however, that some of the work avoidance strategies the child displays could also be due to an underlying specific learning difficulty (dyslexia).

DOI: 10.4324/9781003396796-3

Child C is an autistic child who has had some input on Zones of Regulation in Year 3 on an individual basis. He worked on his toolkit of emotion regulation strategies in Year 3 and in Year 4 with a TA who has a weekly check-in with him, to make sure he remembers how to use those skills.

Child D joined our school at the end of Year 3 from a special school for children with SEMH. He has an EHCP and therefore is entitled to 1:1 support. According to Child E's mum, he has ADHD but a formal diagnosis confirming this has not been received by the school. He does not like to be singled out and given additional support, so help for him has to be across the whole class. In his previous setting, this child struggled to engage with any learning and would often tear up work.

Child E is a very vulnerable child; ours is his third school. For most of Year 3, he was very dysregulated most mornings and found it difficult to stay in the classroom. He started Year 4 in our nurture class in the morning and in his mainstream class for the afternoons.

Child F is the youngest child in his family, with much older siblings. He displays highly oppositional behaviour and struggles to complete tasks even though he does not appear to have any learning needs.

Child G is a very vulnerable child who is under a Child Protection Plan for neglect. He started Year 4 in our nurture class in the morning and in his mainstream class for the afternoons. Recently he also received a diagnosis of dyslexia.

Each child's inability to regulate their emotions had resulted, over time, in there being gaps in learning. This was a vicious circle in that the more learning these children missed by being dysregulated, the more learning gaps developed, meaning they were even less inclined to participate in class.

In addition, the disruption caused by these children had a negative impact on other children's learning and wellbeing. There was a knock-on effect on the class teachers' wellbeing, too, because it was very stressful to manage these children's emotional outbursts, keep everyone safe and teach a whole class.

What we planned

We wanted to implement a programme which would help these children understand the emotions they were feeling, manage their emotions and develop increased empathy for others.

We planned to introduce the Zones of Regulation in both Year 4 classes and in our nurture group. We wanted to support children to be able to reflect after a behaviour issue and eventually enable them to self-reflect before needing adult intervention, managing their emotions and calming themselves before they reach the 'Red' Zone. Children would, we hoped, develop a toolbox of strategies to use as a step-by-step process when feeling unsettled, such as a series of breathing exercises.

To help them self-regulate, we wanted children to have the opportunity to be able to express their emotions and feelings through writing and reflection. We planned for them to have regular emotion check-ins (either with a specific adult, or as part of slots in the class timetable). We also planned time for journalling (we called this a brain dump journal) and time for our 'honouring wall.' Here, children were encouraged to put forward the name of a peer who had been kind, considerate or supportive. The nominated child's name would then go up on the honouring wall, with a brief description of the act of kindness.

How were we influenced by research?

Although we both believed that PSHE was a good thing, it wasn't until we had the opportunity to read about recent SEMH research that we truly understood the benefits of teaching social and emotional skills explicitly.

The Education Endowment Foundation guidance report *Improving Social and Emotional Learning in Primary School* (Van Poortvliet, Clarke and Gross, 2019) clearly explains why social and emotional skills matter, and points to extensive evidence associating well-implemented SEL programmes with both attainment and wellbeing outcomes. It touches on the fact that efforts to promote SEL skills may be especially important for children from disadvantaged backgrounds, who have weaker SEL skills on average, at all ages, than their better-off peers. This research has particular relevance to our context here at Drew.

Another influence on our thinking was the work of Adele Bates. In her book and articles (Bates, 2022) she explains how important it is for us as adults to be able to regulate ourselves and be able to model the techniques to pupils. She talks about the benefits of adults practising self-regulation techniques through short, regular check-ins or by doing something physical. She positively encourages teachers to share their emotions with the children in an appropriate way, and a way they feel comfortable using. We both liked her suggestion of using the register to check in with individuals where children answer the register with one word for how they feel.

'Ready to learn' activities such as free writing were a strategy we were already employing in Year 4, as well as using distraction – for example, asking children to run a quick errand as a means of defusing tensions.

Another source of inspiration was a brilliant Ted Talk by Dr Rosamarie Allen ('School suspensions are an adult behavior', www.youtube.com/watch?v=f8nkcRMZKV4). The talk powerfully illustrates the value of teaching children who don't know to behave, rather than punishing them. We plan to share this video with all staff in forthcoming CPD sessions on SEL.

Jean Gross' suggestions (Gross, 2022) such as hot chocolate breathing and counting forwards or backwards to 10 or 20 were strategies that would become part of our Zones of Regulation toolbox. You can find out more about these in the Resources section of this book.

What we did

We found time in PSHE lessons to introduce the Year 4 children to the Zones of Regulation, following the handbook (Kuypers, 2021), picking and choosing lessons that were appropriate for our timeline and classes.

In our first session we introduced the notion of different colours and zones for various emotions, through the picture book *Conker the Chameleon* by Hannah Peckham. The book describes a world where chameleons have lost the words to explain how they are feeling, but instead show their feelings by changing colour. Poor Conker, however, can't change his colour like the others and is feeling very sad. Then he discovers that what makes him different also makes him special.

The children discussed the book, making a connection to the character of Conker and sharing how they might have felt like Conker at certain times in their lives, and how they felt at different times of the day.

Our second session was an interactive lesson to help children understand the Zones of Regulation through a game of 'emotion bingo' (Figure 3.1).

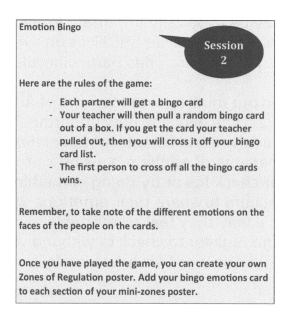

Figure 3.1   Emotion Bingo

The class teacher drew random bingo cards from a box, while the students checked whether they had the same card on their bingo sheet and scratched it off if they had.

The aim of this activity was for the children to closely examine the facial expressions associated with different emotions, noticing subtle differences between one emotion and another. After the game, the children worked in groups to create their own Zones of Regulation poster, using the bingo sheet to arrange the various emotions into the Green, Red, Blue and Yellow Zones.

As the unit of work progressed, we asked the children to watch short clips from films and identify what Zone the characters were in (Figures 3.2 and 3.3).

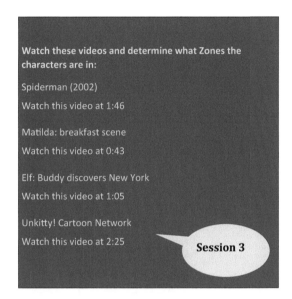

Figure 3.2   Which Zone?

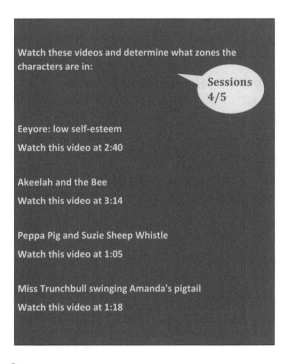

Figure 3.3   Which Zone?

Do you have your Z.O.R. posters?

With your table you are going to add to your poster.

We are going to add the 'toolbox' to each Zone.

Arrange the toolbox according to each Zone.

For example, if you were in the Blue Zone (feeling sleepy and bored) what would you do to help yourself?

Would it help to do some deep breathing or should you be more active and go for a walk?

Figure 3.4   Creating a toolbox of self-regulation strategies

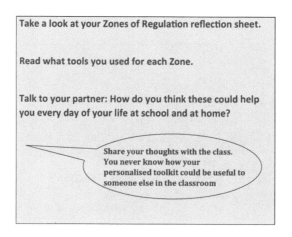

Take a look at your Zones of Regulation reflection sheet.

Read what tools you used for each Zone.

Talk to your partner: How do you think these could help you every day of your life at school and at home?

Share your thoughts with the class. You never know how your personalised toolkit could be useful to someone else in the classroom

Figure 3.5   Sharing our ideas

Thereafter, the students added to their Zones poster by creating a 'toolbox' of self-regulation strategies for each emotion and Zone (Figures 3.4 and 3.5). For example, 'if you are feeling tired, you would be in the Blue Zone, so the tool that could be used would be to go for a walk.' We challenged the children through classroom discussion to be specific about what strategy would be appropriate for each emotion.

At this stage in the process the children became comfortable in our conversation and understanding of the Zones of Regulation. It was therefore time to start implementing it within our classroom. We encouraged children to independently identify their emotions and learn how to move back into the Green Zone to continue learning.

We also introduced a Zones of Regulation display board in our classroom with laminated pictures of each child's face (Figures 3.6 and 3.7). When they arrive at school in the morning they put their picture on whichever Zone they feel they are in. If their emotions have changed throughout the day, they have the opportunity to move their picture again after lunchtime play.

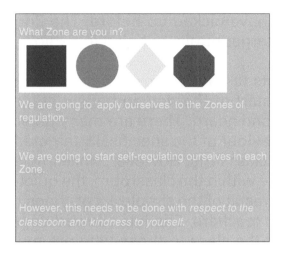

Figure 3.6 Getting ready to use a Zones display

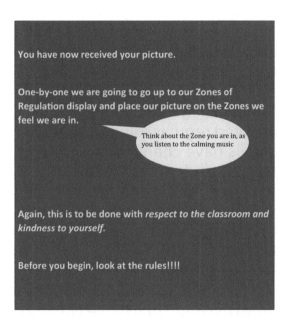

Figure 3.7 Using a Zones display

What we observed

Overall, the work we have done has been a fantastic success within the Year 4 classes as the students have become able to calm themselves when experiencing anger or frustration.

Some students nevertheless still need reminding or encouragement to use the Zones of Regulation display board and to self-regulate.

It has been interesting to observe more reserved students place themselves in a particular Zone when at that moment the class teacher wouldn't have placed them there. For example, there have been times when some of the quietest students in the year group moved their picture to the Red Zone, where we would have never picked up that their emotions were of that intensity. We've also been able to see when they were feeling 'blue', which we would not have picked up before. The Zones has not only been helpful with specific target pupils but also incredibly beneficial for the rest of the class.

Allowing for students to have the opportunity to move their picture from Zone to Zone at the start of the day and again at lunch has given them a platform to feel seen and heard. There are many pupils who often feel overshadowed by the behaviour of the specifically targeted children, who mostly take up attention and class time. However, since implementing the Zones of Regulation as a routine within the classroom, the quieter children's emotions are literally seen, as a result of the simple act of choosing where to place their picture. As classroom teachers, this has allowed us to shift our focus from dominant students in the class to those who are more reserved and need emotional support.

When we have noticed children (who aren't the target pupils) are in the yellow, red, or Blue Zone we have made the effort to pull them aside and ask, 'Are you okay?', 'Do you need to talk about it?', 'Did something happen at school, in the classroom, or playground?.' As a result, we have been able to identify other pupils within the classroom who may need emotional support and, in some cases, encouraged them to self-refer to Place2Talk or referred them to Place2Be for counselling.

We have also implemented regular mindfulness after break time and again after lunch (after the pupils have changed their picture for the second time). This is done by waiting for students to be seated in a 'mindfulness-ready' position, which includes feet flat on the ground, spine straight, shoulders relaxed, palms facing upwards and eyes closed. We complete a series of four cycles of deep 'belly-breathing', allowing for emotions to calm and neutrality to be brought to the body.

Our class teachers involved in the project all modelled self-regulation and found this technique beneficial to our students. On a day-to-day basis, they would model moving from the Red Zone to the Green Zone independently. For example, 'I am feeling really frustrated right now, and I need to use my toolbox to self-regulate so that I can get into the Green Zone and continue with my day.' The teachers would then demonstrate using a mindfulness technique.

Impact

One of our data comparisons was the number of behaviour incidents logged for our focus group of children in the Autumn term '21 (before Zones of Regulation were introduced), and in the summer term '22 (after Zones were introduced).

Year 4 classes: Total number of behaviour logs (9-week period)

	Autumn term	Summer term
Regents Park Class	36	24
Hyde Park Class	47	31

Focus group of Year 4: Total number of behaviour logs (9-week period)

	Autumn term	Summer term
Child A	14	3
Child B	0	0
Child C	0	0
Child D	21	16
Child E	4	0
Child F	3	6
Child G	4	2

From the reduction in behaviour incidents for most of the children in the focus group, we feel that our work has had a positive effect. Using the Leuven Scale to quantify observation data, we were also able to see that there had been an improvement in most of the focus group's wellbeing.

Despite these positive findings, we are very aware of the limitations of our mini research project. The numbers of children in our focus group are very small. A couple of children, originally chosen, could not be included (one did not receive parental consent and another child left at Christmas).

There were changes in home circumstances for some children, over which we had no control, but which will have affected their wellbeing. For others, there were changes in school such as a change of 1:1 TA support which may also have had an impact.

For some individuals we can feel confident that introducing Zones of Regulation was a contributing factor to improved behaviour and wellbeing. However, for other children in the focus group, outside factors were clearly at play and the project did not have an impact on their self-regulation.

Changes to learning behaviours

We cannot ignore the fact that this would be the first full school year that these children have had in the last two years due to COVID-19. A vast majority of the children find it hard to persevere with their learning, struggling to concentrate as the year progresses. The workload seems overwhelming and it is very evident which children regularly participate in home learning and those who do not. The lack of stamina has greatly affected the lesson outcomes and assessment data. For example, we did a recap unit of subtraction at the start of the year, and as we bring it up through revision, the students need constant reminders on how to answer the equation.

Nevertheless, we found positive changes in children's learning behaviours when we interviewed a range of staff to ask for their observations on any changes they had seen within the classroom.

The learning mentor who is in one class for English every day noticed that the classroom is a calmer environment, where the children are less needy and have become more independent. The pupils have learned that it is 'okay to feel whatever you are feeling', which has encouraged an acceptance of differences. They know that it is alright to be at different levels than their peers (in both emotions and learning).

PE lessons can result in children becoming over-excited and not ready for learning. Our PE teacher has observed positive incremental changes as a result of the work we have all done, noticing that children are starting to manage their own emotions and respond to situations with more appropriate behaviour. He said that in some children he has seen an immense change, while others are still working towards it.

The music teacher has observed that when he enters the classroom, the Zones of Regulation displays help him manage specific children, as it gives a clear indication of where they are at emotionally and how they should be approached. He commented that behaviour issues in class often have a ripple effect, so when the class is being managed as a whole through mindfulness and the Zones check-in, this can have a positive effect on the learning and the lesson.

We have observed that, overall, children have become more resilient in their attitude towards learning, but aware that factors other than the SEL work we did could have contributed to this – factors such as undertaking different units of work, general increases in maturity and growth within children's foundational understanding of the Year 4 curriculum.

Individual children who struggle with work in general have become more able to manage their emotions when they cannot understand something. Some students have shifted from becoming irritated and agitated to being more patient with themselves and their ability to work through their emotions has benefited their learning.

Working with parents

We have mentioned our implementation of the Zones of Regulation in PSHE in our year group newsletter. It has also been brought up casually in parents' evening consultations. However, we recently sent a Parent Mail formally informing the parents about our approach.

A few weeks after encouraging parents to use the Zones of Regulation vocabulary at home, we plan to send out a survey on Google Forms, asking them to share with us any impact (positive or negative) the Zones of Regulation programme might have had at home.

Wider school impact

We introduced the Big Education project to our school in several ways. First, we explained our plans in a staff briefing, then we had a 10-minute presentation during one of our CPD sessions. In this session we explained the project in more detail, focusing particularly on our research topic: 'Will teaching self-regulation skills have an impact on emotional wellbeing?'

We invited our colleagues to give feedback or helpful tips. In the staffroom, we left an information poster with an envelope and post-its for suggestions, thoughts or advice for the staff to comment on.

Later we ran a twilight session to explain the Zones of Regulation to the entire body of staff. This presented a wonderful opportunity for teachers to engage in discussions, ask questions about how it worked in Year 4, as well as discuss with their partner teacher how they think it could work within their own year groups or classes. The majority of the staff were engaged and eager to learn about managing behaviour by using Zones every day within the classroom. Our learning mentors use the Zones of Regulation with specific students and their expertise, knowledge and years of experience have made their advice incredibly helpful.

Our twilight session for staff demonstrated exactly how the Zones could be taught within the classroom.

In a longer presentation we explained to staff how successful Zones can be as part of our Positive Behaviour management and Emotion Coaching techniques. We were keen to demonstrate how all these strategies complement one another.

After the twilight session in the summer of 2022, a small number of teachers introduced Zones in their classes in September. In addition, the teacher of our nurture group and our learning mentors introduced Zones of Regulation with some children from across the school, in small group and 1:1 sessions.

Now, six months later, the Zones of Regulation have been introduced across the whole school, led by our new Headteacher.

What lessons could other schools draw from your experiences?

Looking at our experience, another school may see that finding out about recent research is essential before embarking on a change. They may see the benefits of trying out a new programme or set of strategies with a pilot group initially, before then attempting to get others on board.

Historically, our school has a reputation for constantly bringing in new ideas and methods of work, which can be exhausting for staff. Going into this research project, we were conscious of teacher workload as well as the problems associated with 'shoe-horning' more and more activities into an already full curriculum.

Quite rightly, when we start a new project, staff often ask 'What do we drop?' However, because we have used an evidence-based intervention and begun with a pilot group in our own school, staff have been more open-minded about the possible benefits. They know we have tested a new idea in our own particular context – not with children from a different demographic or in a different socio-economic area. They also know that two class-based teachers are available to support them and bring practical experience of successes and potential pitfalls.

Other schools may decide to look into the benefits of introducing a programme such as Zones of Regulation but might also learn from our experience that for some children with complex SEMH needs, a programme such as Zones needs to be complemented by more intense support and/or counselling.

Reflections

We have learned a great deal from our work on this project.

From a teacher's perspective, the whole approach to the Zones of Regulation has given me an insight into my students – particularly those who are shy and tend to not be as vocal. A light has shifted onto them where their emotions feel seen and heard, even if they are still silent.

Overall, I have learnt that each child has a complexity of emotions that can sometimes stay dormant, or at other times lead to an eruption. Some students allow their emotions to bubble for a long time, leading to a surprising boil-over. Regardless of how each child is feeling emotionally, they need to be treated and dealt with on an individual basis. They need to be nurtured and taught how to find their way back to the Green Zone with small actions – the simplest of acts: taking a breath, closing your eyes, giving a hug, talking softly.

I myself have become calmer by practising mindfulness and the Zones of Regulation, as I am able to demonstrate how to centre myself before I begin teaching - which sets the class on an even note.

(Teacher)

It has been very rewarding seeing how the teacher's confidence in managing the children's behaviour has grown. I am also particularly heartened by the fact this project has given an opportunity for the quieter children to be noticed and have their emotional needs met.

I have learnt that social, emotional, learning skills need to be taught explicitly. SEL does not happen 'by osmosis' and it is important to use a planned series of lessons in dedicated time. I found it is essential to regularly review progress in discussion with classroom practitioners and to problem-solve as a group.

My understanding of SEL has deepened. I learnt how Zones of Regulation can work when implemented consistently and can benefit many children at a universal level. However, I saw at first hand that for some pupils' self-regulation is a much bigger issue. For pupils who have experienced trauma, abuse and neglect or have mental health problems there may be long-term issues that mean they are unable to self-regulate, as others do. The whole process will take longer, need to be more personalised, targeted and, in many cases, the child may need specialist support.

(Leader)

Key takeaways

- The Zones of Regulation should be introduced slowly and step-by-step.
- It is crucial that students are aware that being in the red, yellow or Blue Zones is not wrong.
- It is important that the children feel seen and heard.
- Use the Zones within your own vocabulary as you go through the day.
- The Zones is NOT the same as a behaviour chart. It shouldn't be discussed as one and the same.
- As a teacher, the Zones can be used for you to check in where your children are at.
- The Zones will help you identify the 'under the radar' students.

4 The upstairs and downstairs brain
Learning about neuroscience at New City Primary

Eilidh Kirkpatrick and Annabel Greyling

Just like Drew Primary School in the last chapter, we based a lot of our work on teaching children to use the Zones of Regulation. We began this, though, by teaching children some basic neuroscience and also teaching them to use a technique called 'the size of the problem' to help them handle tricky situations and uncomfortable feelings. Here we explain why, and how we went about it.

The children

We too chose to focus our work on Year 4 pupils as they had a higher number of recorded 'reflection times' (behaviour incidents that were escalated from the class teacher to a member of the Senior Leadership Team) than other year groups in the first term of the 21/22 academic year.

Year Group	Number of 'reflection times' in Autumn 1 term
1	1
2	0
3	2
4	10
5	3
6	6

When we looked into the reasons for these reflection times, pupils seemed to be emotional and lashing out at other pupils (both verbally and physically), throwing objects in class or damaging school property.

- Attempted to strangle a child by pulling her top
- Told K to hurt H … used words 'destroy her'
- For talking over the teacher and throwing equipment in class

DOI: 10.4324/9781003396796-4

The pupils' class teachers said that the children seemed calm before the incident but their behaviour and emotional state quickly deteriorated. This suggested to us that perhaps emotions were building up over the day, to the point where pupils 'lost it.' None of the children involved had been given a reflection more than twice in the first half term, suggesting their behaviour had been generally good. We wondered if these children fell into the group described in Chapter 1, who are generally able to follow behavioural expectations and appear to engage well with learning but have irregular days where their emotions seem to overwhelm them and they act out in unacceptable ways.

Each class teacher in our Year 4 cohort reported that overall they found the classes they were teaching this year became upset or angry more quickly than other classes in the same year group they have previously taught. One teacher suggested that this might be because of COVID-19: Year 4 pupils had not had a full year of school since they were in Year 1 and missed out not only on key learning within our PSHE curriculum related to emotional regulation, but also on socialisation opportunities in which to practise and embed these skills.

> *This year they are … they are more emotional. They seem more immature and get upset or like angry about little things.*
>
> *Maybe it's because this is their first full year of school since they were like.. Year … 1? It's a lot of school to miss.*

(Year 4 class teachers)

We gathered baseline data on the Year 4 cohort using our school behaviour logs, a Leuven Questionnaire and Experience at School Survey.

The results of the Leuven teacher-completed questionnaire suggested that at least a quarter of the year group had issues with engagement and well-being, and difficulties in relation to emotions, concentration, behaviour and ability to get on with one other. Nevertheless, the majority of pupils in Year 4 engaged in high (33%) or extremely high levels of involvement (34%) within their classroom, suggesting good engagement with learning. We wondered whether specific children place a burden on themselves or the rest of the class due to school pressures to manage difficult behaviour and to promote an exceptionally high standard of learning that engages all pupils.

On the Experience at School Survey (a self-report measure completed anonymously by pupils) we found that our children were in the average range of wellbeing (58th centile) overall. A notable finding, however, was that many pupils did not feel relaxed at school, had feelings of tiredness and also felt confused.

Feelings of 'not feeling relaxed' and being 'tired' could be pupil reactions to the high behavioural expectations at New City. It could also be speculated that the confusion felt by pupils might relate to lack of self-awareness and ability to manage their emotions.

Clearly the behaviour log data and the Leuven scales results showed that a substantial proportion of our Year 4 pupils could benefit from learning how better to manage stress and uncomfortable emotions, so it made sense to implement the Zones of Regulation approach. We also wanted to address the feelings of confusion reported by pupils. Drawing on the idea that feelings of anxiety about where thoughts and feelings come from can be reduced through teaching children about basic neuroscience, we also drew on Dan Siegel's metaphors of the 'Upstairs' and 'Downstairs' brain (Siegel and Pane Bryson, 2011) and began the first stage of our explicit social and emotional teaching with a lesson on 'Flipping the lid.' You can find this lesson and those that followed in the Resources section of this book.

There is also a very useful BBC PSHE programme for schools about these ideas, which you can find at www.bbc.co.uk/teach/class-clips-video/pshe-ks2-the-brain-house/zd7kd6f.

What we did

We developed a series of lessons, beginning with the lesson on basic neuroscience then weekly, explicit, social and emotional learning lessons focused on identifying and managing the emotions in each of the Zones of Regulation (Figures 4.1 and 4.2).

Figure 4.1   What you see, fear, hear

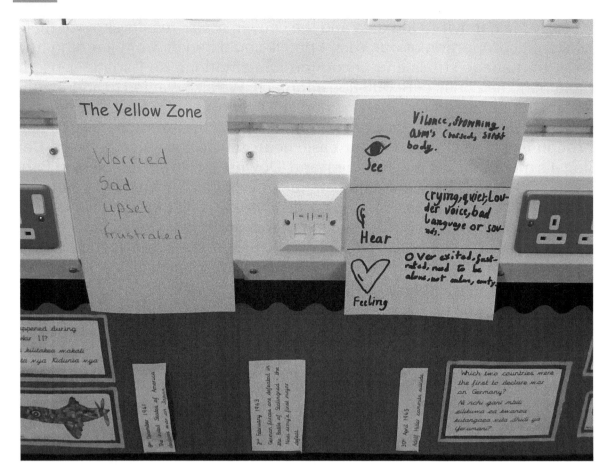

Figure 4.2   What you see, fear, hear

Each lesson was based around a story or book suggested in the 'Zones Book Nook', which you can find online at https://zonesofregulation.com/zones-book-nook.html.

Some of the books we used were *When Sophie Gets Angry* by Mollie Bang, *A Little Spot of Sadness* by Diane Alber, *The Good Egg* by Jory John and Pete Oswald, *The Invisible Boy* by Trudy Ludwig and Patrice Barton, *Clark the Shark* by Bruce Hale, *Sweep* by Louise Greig, *Millie Fierce* by Jane Manning and *Sam's Pet Temper* by Sangeeta Bhadra. We used the stories to identify which zones the characters were in and to explore how they moved from Zone to Zone, with their own strategies for moving into the Green Zone (Figures 4.3, 4.4 and 4.5).

We began each explicit 'Zones' lesson with private reflection and interaction with our Zones of Regulation display chart (Figure 4.6).

Once the children were confident in recognising the Zones and strategies to up- and down-regulate we introduced work on the 'size of the problem' (Figure 4.7). This is another approach originally used with autistic children (www.socialthinking.com). Children are taught to rate the size of any problem we face from tiny through small, medium and large, according to how dangerous the problematic event is, how long it will last, the number of people involved and how difficult it is to solve.

The teachers taught these 30-minute lessons every week for a 12-week period (one full term). Our Headteacher made sure there would be protected space within the Year 4 timetable.

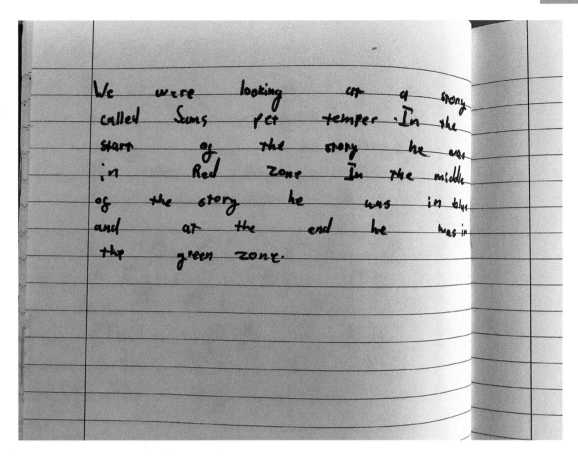

Figure 4.3 Sam's pet temper

Figure 4.4 Moving from the Blue Zone

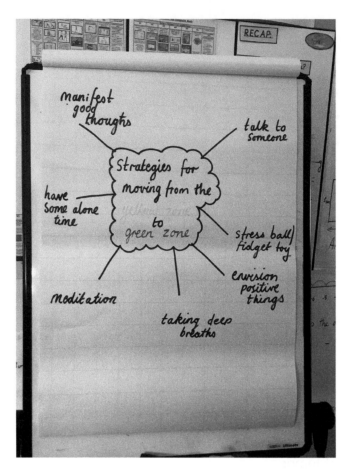

Figure 4.5   Moving from the yellow Zone

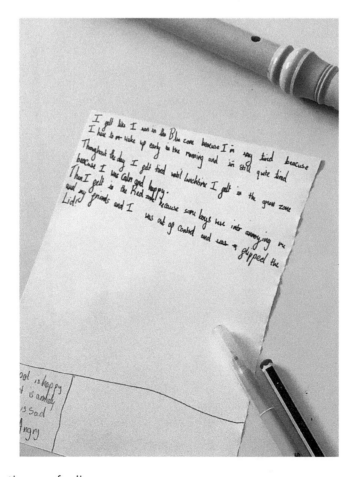

Figure 4.6   Reflecting on feelings

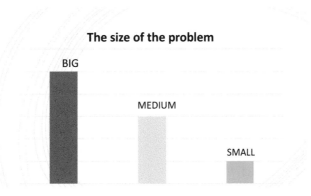

Figure 4.7   The size of the problem

Figure 4.8   Zones display

We created a Zones of Regulation display (Figure 4.8) in each class which the children could interact with and move their name to display how they were feeling. The aim of this was to allow the teachers to refer to and encourage pupil engagement with the Zones during everyday teaching, as well as during the explicit lessons.

Whilst the explicit lessons were successful, teachers reported that they had struggled to embed using the Zones display emotional check-in board into daily practice, and that they often referred to it more if they felt a child was disrupting the class. We felt this was perhaps encouraging shame linked to different emotions and was not the most positive strategy. On reflection, we feel it would have been better to introduce set times of the day (e.g. morning and afternoon register, before breaks and lunches) to 'check in' with pupils.

The impact

Data collected from the Leuven Wellbeing scale showed an overall improvement after the work we did, with a 17% increase in teachers reporting high or extremely high child wellbeing. The number of pupils expressing difficulties with emotions, concentration, behaviour and being able to get on with others fell from 10% (October) to 6% (May). Pupils reported similar levels of sadness post-intervention. However, there was a decrease in 'I wanted to cry', suggesting they are regulating their emotions before they reached a critical level. There was also a decrease in the numbers of pupils feeling confused. It could be argued that this is due to increased awareness and understanding of their emotions.

Information from the Experience at School Survey suggested an increase in pro-social behaviours and a decrease in some anti-social behaviours. A downward trend in 'reflection times' or behavioural incidents was also evident. In our first half term of the academic year before our project began, Year 4 had 10 reflections in the first half term. After 12 weeks of the project, this had decreased to six.

Unfortunately, we also saw an increase in reported bullying behaviours – being a victim, but not self-reporting as a perpetrator of bullying. This could suggest that the bullying was coming from other year groups, who share playgrounds with the Year 4s and did not take part in our intervention. It might also explain the decrease in 'school satisfaction' we found.

When it came to an impact on attainment, we found slight improvements across the year group in maths, with an increase of five percentage points in pupils working at expected or greater depth level by the end of May 2022 in comparison with our October 2021 data. There was also a four-percentage point increase in pupils working at expected or greater depth in their writing during this time period, but no change to reading scores.

Teachers commented on improvements to children's learning behaviours, with pupils more able to stay focused.

> Children have improved in their concentration and are aware of strategies they can use when they are feeling in a different zone. They are using the zones to show how they are feeling and moving it when their emotions have changed.

(Year 4 class teachers)

We also saw encouraging signs of children using the strategies in their life outside school (Figure 4.9).

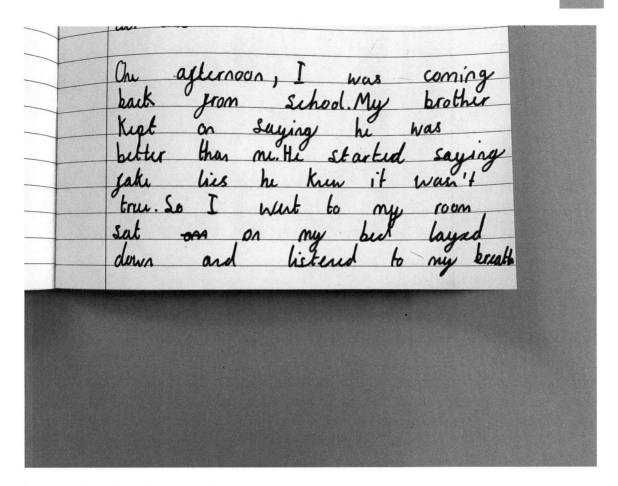

One afternoon, I was coming back from school. My brother Kept on saying he was better than me. He started saying fake lies he knew it wasn't true. So I went to my room sat on my bed layed down and listened to my breath

Figure 4.9   Using the strategies

Wider school impact and next steps

We held a staff meeting and shared the results of our intervention so far with the wider teaching staff. We were well supported by our Headteacher who articulated the change she had personally seen in the Year 4 pupils.

Our primary challenge during the project was maintaining teacher enthusiasm for the intervention and drive to use the Zones within everyday practice. Through discussion with our behaviour lead, we therefore planned that when we launched the Zones across the whole school in the next academic year, our senior leadership team (SLT) would build teacher use of an interactive Zones display into their teacher observation sheet. We hoped that seeing the 'check-ins' are valued and approved by SLT will encourage regular use and that it will, with time, become standard practice for our teachers.

To support colleagues, we planned two lessons that they could use to introduce the Zones. The first observation has now taken place, four weeks into the new school year.

Children are now able to have their own self-regulation 'toolbox' on their desk, to remind them of the strategies that work best for them.

We have made lanyards for our midday supervisors to use to help children show how they are feeling and use strategies to self-regulate and resolve conflicts in the playground (Figures 4.10, 4.11 and 4.12).

Figures 4.10, 4.11 and 4.12   Lanyards
© Widgit Software Ltd 2002–2023

We have also worked with our school's three earning mentors and school counsellor to ensure consistent language and approaches to SEL across the school. The learning mentors now have an interactive Zones display in their room – the room to which children are sent by midday supervisors if behaviour issues can't be resolved. We made up a pack about the Zones for these colleagues, including the board games that are suggested in Leah Kuypers' book (Kuypers, 2021). Soon, we hope that the learning mentors will offer additional targeted group support for children who need extra help with their social and emotional learning.

We are also planning to meet with parents to introduce the Zones and how they can be used at home, and next year intend to plan a progression in social and emotional learning to embed into our PSHE curriculum.

Key takeaways

- It is important to provide teachers with dedicated time for social and emotional learning within their timetable, rather than asking them to squeeze it in alongside other obligations.
- It is helpful to teach children some basic neuroscience, to help them understand how their emotions work.
- Schedule fixed times in the day for emotion check-ins, rather than using them when problems arise.
- Work as a team, involving everyone in school, including lunchtime supervisors.

5 How we solved playground problems at Cubitt Town Primary

Emma Whitwam and Jessica Robinson

The children

Our target pupils were two classes, Year 3 and Year 6. We were concerned about the impact of COVID-19 on their social communication. We were particularly concerned about how they were able to recognise and regulate their emotions, and how this impacted problems in the playground.

Playground conflict is a normal part of social development, but the extent of the problems in both Year 3 and Year 6 was impacting children's happiness and focus on learning. Problems filtered into the classroom and meant children were not ready to learn in the afternoon. We were concerned about the impact this was having on their attainment.

We observed that children seemed to have very few conflict resolution strategies. Our data showed us that within the Year 3 class, children's only strategy was to tell an adult. They therefore relied heavily on adult support to deal with their problems. In contrast, in the Year 6 class, children would tend to ignore the problem and the person involved and not deal with the problem. They had some conflict resolution strategies but they were not well used.

Our context and strategy

Children's social, emotional and mental health and wellbeing is a cornerstone of our school and one of the strands of our school development plan, alongside raising attainment.

Another of our school's key drivers is oracy. Children take part in a variety of scaffolded activities to improve their spoken language skills. We measure the impact of this work on the four strands of oracy: physical, linguistic, cognitive and social/emotional. We anticipated that if we provided scaffolds to help children talk through playground problems, this would contribute to progress in the social/emotional oracy strand.

By teaching and scaffolding conflict resolution, we felt that children's wellbeing would improve: they would be happier due to being better at managing their feelings and maintaining friendships.

DOI: 10.4324/9781003396796-5

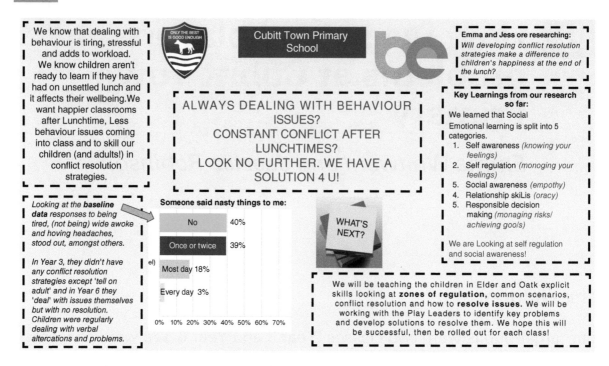

Figure 5.1   The problem and the strategy

To clarify our thinking about our project, and communicate information about the programme to other staff in school, we created a poster (Figure 5.1) setting out an analysis of the problem and our strategy to tackle it.

What we learned from research

From our literature review, we learned that teaching children explicit social and emotional strategies positively impacts their wellbeing and that there are five strands of SEL (Van Poortvliet, Clarke and Gross, 2019).

This prompted us to think about which of these strands we needed to focus on, in order to best support our learners. From our data collection, we became aware that social awareness and self-management was an area that was lacking in our children and needed to be addressed, as children could identify their emotions, but were not confident in strategies to regulate and manage them. They also did not display empathy in conflict scenarios. Our literature review highlighted that we needed to explicitly teach children how to manage and regulate their emotions and teach them empathy, through role-play.

The evident lack of self-management in children encouraged us to think of how we could get children to identify where they were in terms of feelings and what they needed to do to support themselves. Analysing a range of literature helped us decide to focus on teaching the Zones of Regulation (Kuypers, 2021) in order to develop children's ability to manage their feelings when they were angry, upset or anxious.

By discussing the Zones with the children we acknowledged the need for us as teachers to say how we are feeling at emotion check-ins, and model this truthfully to the children. As well as being useful for adults to self-regulate and monitor themselves, we realised the impact this would have on the class (Bates, 2021). We learned about using explicit emotion check-ins (Gross, 2021) and drew on research on co-regulation (Desautels, 2019).

Desautels' research also highlighted that children who had a 'buddy' in school were able to co-regulate with someone they trust in a safe environment. Therefore, we decided to create a Year 3 and 6 'buddy system' for children to support each other's social, emotional and mental health needs.

We have learned that validating pupils when they are feeling upset and angry can help bring calmness and a sense of understanding (Desautels, 2019). From other sources (Gross, 2021) we learned about the benefits of teaching children appropriate vocabulary to identify emotions so that they can 'name it to tame it' (Siegel, 2014).

We were interested in why some of our children struggled to regulate their emotions and found the model that Jean Gross has described in Chapter 1 of particular value. She describes four main reasons for behaviour problems; we wanted to focus on children who 'can't behave because they don't know how to' – because they lack the SEL skills (such as self-regulation) that underpin positive behaviour.

Changes to teaching

From the data, we realised we needed to split our project into two parts based on our understanding of SEL as outlined by the Education Endowment Foundation. First, we needed to teach emotional regulation and second, we needed to teach social communication on the playground.

From understanding that our project needed to be two-fold, we devised an intervention to run weekly in Year 3 and Year 6. Initially, we taught a series of discrete oracy sessions around emotional regulation. These were 20-minute sessions and taught the Zones of Regulation (Figure 5.2) alongside looking at common playground problems. These happened at the same time each week, within our Personal, Social and Health Education (PSHE) time.

Changes to pastoral care

Proactive and compassionate pastoral care is crucial in our school and we are lucky to work in a setting that puts pupils' wellbeing at front and centre of learning. From this research project, we have added additional elements of pastoral care for the pupils in Years 3 and 6.

One of the first steps we took was to update how children 'check in' with how they are feeling in the day, by upgrading our old system of 'how are you feeling today?' to Zones of Regulation. We explicitly modelled how to use the Zones, demonstrated how our Zones can vary throughout the day and emphasised that no Zone is 'bad.' Zones of Regulation were used throughout the day and children have created and tailored their own Zones charts with specific strategies that help them to self-regulate. In Year 6, a 'Zen Zone' was introduced (Figure 5.3), where a large 'Zone of Regulation' was displayed for pupils to see. We provided bean bags, cushions and blankets to ensure comfort for the children, while they were regulating.

Figure 5.2   A Zones of Regulation display

Figure 5.3   Zen Zone

Additionally, we have ensured that this area is accessible to all children, by providing ear defenders and objects to smell and touch. The area also has a range of fiction and non-fiction texts relating to social, emotional and mental health. In line with the importance of developing a culture of readers, another book display of wellbeing books around managing mental health was erected near the Year 3 classrooms.

Through implementing Zones of Regulation displays and specific 'Zen Zone' areas, we have seen children proactively take themselves to a safe space to calm down before returning to class. Children have also been borrowing books from the wellbeing book displays and sharing them with their friends. We have seen greater empathy in the children in Year 6; when a child is in the 'Zen Zone', a friend will often ask if they can go and check in with them, especially if they have spent longer than five minutes there.

A second change we have made in our pastoral provision was creating a buddy system to promote co-regulation amongst our children, so that they had someone else they could talk to and trust. This has proved helpful for children who have been reluctant to speak to adults, or come forward with issues. The buddy system has been particularly effective in the Year 3 cohort, as children are proactively seeking out their Year 6 buddy to talk to them about how they are feeling. In turn, this has created greater social awareness amongst Year 6s, as they are listening to and supporting Year 3 in nurturing and positive ways.

A third change in our pastoral care was in playground systems. From our qualitative data, we acknowledged that Play Leaders (midday meal supervisors) needed training around conflict resolution. After we had embedded Zones of Regulation within our classrooms, we held a training session for our Play Leaders, in which we explicitly taught them about the Zones and how our children were using them. We also introduced the supervisors to the 'Cubitt Town Peace Path' (Figure 5.4) which we were about to introduce to the children, to give them a way of solving playground conflicts in a safe, non-blaming way. We gave the Play Leaders the opportunity to read through the strategies, ask questions and practise the strategies. They were given copies to have with them in the playground, so as to coach children to use the sequence of steps.

In class we introduced the 'Peace Path' to provide children with a systematic, oracy-based sequence to follow when issues came up. We had an oracy assembly with Year 3 and Year 6 and the Play Leaders, where we used drama to practise the Peace Path techniques. Older children practised the sequence with their Year 3 buddies. This part of the intervention was highly successful and had excellent engagement from students and teachers alike. The older buddies loved helping their younger buddies and they had a shared topic of interest.

The impact: changes to learning behaviours

There have been some notable changes in our cohorts, as a result of our work. Children in Years 3 and 6 are calmer and more often feel 'in the Green Zone.' From the Year 3 and Year 6 oracy assembly, we heard the children in both year groups using a wide range of emotional vocabulary. Children were using language such as envious, frustrated, irritated, as well as angry

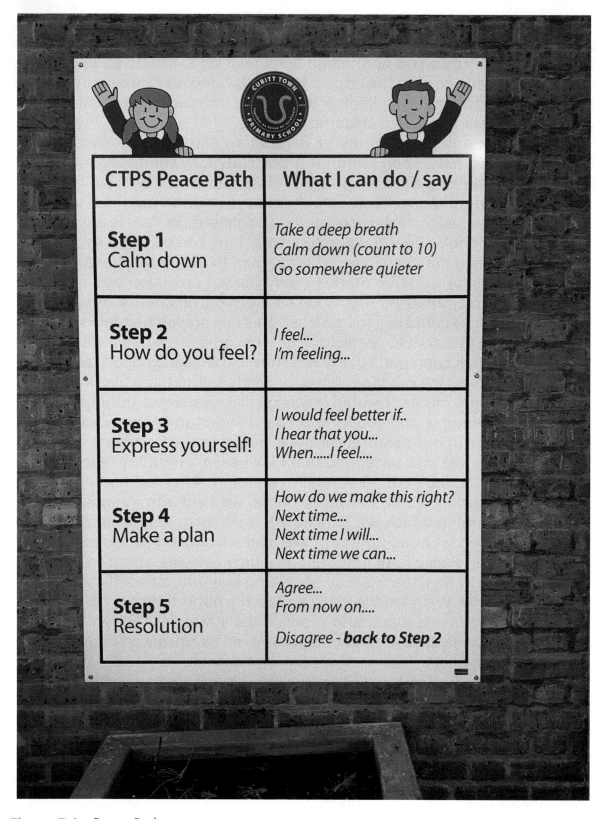

Figure 5.4   Peace Path

and were able to associate them with the correct Zone. They were also able to understand that some emotions might co-occur across two Zones, or that one feeling (for example anger) might be the result of another feeling (for example, embarrassment).

Children in both classes can now use the Zones to understand their own emotions, but also to regulate their emotions more readily. This is apparent in the data collected from the Leuven Scale, as Year 6 children had an increase of 0.7 points in relation to observing their wellbeing (4.3 on average in May, compared to 3.6 on average in the previous November).

As well as better emotional regulation, we have found that playground issues are not taking up as much time in class after playtimes. Children had better empathy towards each other, which was particularly apparent when we introduced the buddies. Our observations are supported by Leuven Scale data, where we saw an increase of 0.3 in relation to Year 6 children's involvement in lessons (4.1 average in May, compared to 3.8 average in November). Children are better equipped to resolve conflict, but they are also more able to articulate their problem using dialogue before they get frustrated. They have started using conflict resolution strategies; for example, in Year 6, we have seen children using the 'Zen Zone' after lunch with the person they have had an issue with and once calm, both children have talked through the issue and made up their quarrel.

Children have responded really well to having a buddy. Those in Year 3 were quoted as saying 'I love my buddy', 'we have loads in common' and they are actively seeking out their buddy in the playground. The Year 6 children are now more nurturing towards the younger children at playtimes, as before they used to become irritated by having to share playtimes with them (after a year of segregated playtimes due to COVID restrictions). We have observed Year 6 children helping Year 3, by taking them to an adult in the playground if they have had an issue that they cannot resolve on their own, or if they have hurt themselves. This buddy system has had a really beneficial impact on all children's safety and enjoyment of the playground.

The training for Play Leaders has led to observable changes in their behaviours. Before the training, they would often try to 'solve' children's problems and deal with issues on behalf of a child. Now they understand the importance of children developing social and communication skills to manage emotions and conflict. The Play Leaders have been proactive in supporting our project and have commented that they found the training 'purposeful and achievable.' As teachers, we have noticed the Play Leaders are dealing with playground issues using communication and modelling empathy.

We hope that over time, as our project becomes more embedded, we will see evidence of less adult intervention from the Play Leaders, as children will be using the 'Peace Path' strategy independently to solve problems.

We have found that children with social, emotional and mental health (SEMH) needs and SEND have benefited greatly from this intervention, but that children who we would not expect to have benefited have also gained from and enjoyed the intervention. For example, one of our quieter Year 3s has developed much greater confidence since starting this project.

The senior leadership team have highlighted 'the culture of wellbeing' in their classroom observations of Year 3 and Year 6. With further rollout, we would anticipate this to be spread across the school.

Despite not specifically involving parents, we have had some positive feedback from them about children being 'more settled' and 'more confident.' At the end of the project we plan to send parents a summary of our findings and what students have learned. Some of our parents are Play Leaders, so for them it has been very impactful as colleagues, but they have also been able to apply some of these strategies at home. Moving forward, we would also like to offer Zones of Regulation training to families, so that they can use this tool at home.

Wider school impact

In the academic year following our project we introduced Zones of Regulation across the school and are using them alongside our emotional check-ins. The Peace Path on the playground is starting to be used in all of KS2 with the aim to introduce it in KS1 in the summer term.

Factors that have enabled us to move towards a whole-school approach were:

- sharing our project and its impact with staff as we went along and at the end of the project.
- including a member of middle leadership (Senior Mental Health Lead and PSHE Lead) in the project – this enabled the work to have greater influence.
- timing – our work coincided well with a newly written PSHE curriculum where we could incorporate the new practices.
- involving the Play Leaders in the early stages as key stakeholders, which created a positive relationship that we hope will sustain long-lasting change on the playground.
- the opportunity to pilot the scheme across two year groups first. This has been beneficial as we can go to other staff with a working model and ready-made resources. We have also been able to demonstrate the impact we have already seen by implementing the change. Working from the top of the school with Year 6 has shown that the model works in Upper Key Stage 2 and can be modified for younger year groups. Alongside this, completing the project in Year 3 has allowed us to consider what changes would be necessary for a successful introduction in Key Stage 1.

Key takeaways

- Invest time – in staff, pupils and PSHE learning.
- Take time to gather qualitative pupil voice and use that to address real issues in PSHE sessions.
- Set time aside each week to address social and emotional needs, so as to create a culture of children who feel safe to share emotions and develop their knowledge about how to look after their mental health.
- Identify and invest time in key stakeholders (for us, that was our Play Leaders), and listen to their views.
- Use the power of peer support, such as buddy systems, which build empathy and allow for co-regulation.

6 How we helped withdrawn children come out of their shells at Selwyn Primary

Laura Partington and Susan Potter

Our context

At the start of the academic year, our leadership team decided that it was a school priority to raise the profile of wellbeing and the understanding of SEMH in our school.

We already had a focus on promoting pupil wellbeing through staff training on restorative practice and attachment theory, through our use of Place2Be services, through the work of our Emotional Literacy Support Assistant (ELSA) and through mental and physical health learning within our Relationships and Health curriculum (Figure 6.1). However, we wanted to develop some practical tools that could be used in classes to replace strategies that previously had not been successful.

A previous needs analysis had shown us that we should focus on children talking about their emotions as part of a restorative approach to behaviour and self-regulation. The concept of a 'colour register' based on the book The Colour Monster had been introduced, so children could say how they were feeling during morning and afternoon registrations. However, this was not embedded across the school because teachers were not consistently using the strategies and the children did not have a clear understanding of how to identify their own emotions. They often just responded 'rainbow.' Children's responses were not always followed up. A new approach was needed that would be scalable across the school and which could be adapted for different year groups.

The plan

Instead of rolling out a new approach in all classes straight away, we decided to start with one Year 3 class. We chose to focus on children who were more reserved and less confident in a whole-class setting. Academically, these children performed variably (some working towards the expected standard with others working at age-related expectations). Their behaviours included being unable to accept praise, lacking greatly in confidence and being very shy and reluctant to participate in whole-class discussions or group work.

DOI: 10.4324/9781003396796-6

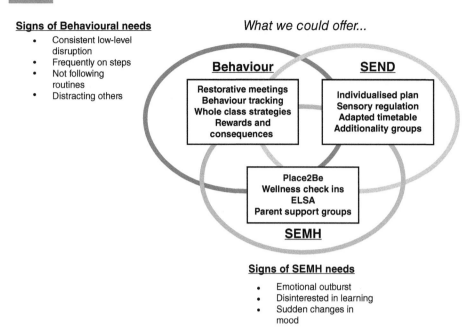

Signs of Behavioural needs
- Consistent low-level disruption
- Frequently on steps
- Not following routines
- Distracting others

What we could offer...

Behaviour
Restorative meetings
Behaviour tracking
Whole class strategies
Rewards and consequences

SEND
Individualised plan
Sensory regulation
Adapted timetable
Additionality groups

Place2Be
Wellness check ins
ELSA
Parent support groups

SEMH

Signs of SEND needs
- Difficulties in accessing learning
- Difficulties in transitions
- Disengaged with rest of the class
- Short attention span

Signs of SEMH needs
- Emotional outburst
- Disinterested in learning
- Sudden changes in mood

Figure 6.1   The school's offer

We used the Happiness Scale to help us understand these children's needs. What we found, however, was that they were unable to articulate their feelings or to describe the feelings that other children in their class might have. One pupil responded 'everyone in my class is happy.' Another pupil struggled to respond with any name when asked who they thought was the unhappiest child in the class. Despite being in a class with children with behaviour difficulties and SEND needs, our focus pupils struggled to identify their own feelings and the feelings of others in their class.

This insight helped us to decide to focus our work on strategies to promote emotional intelligence – the ability to understand, identify and express feelings and emotions (Nikolajeva, 2013; Schiller, 2009).

What we learned from research and reading

We learned from the EEF guidance (Van Poortvliet, Clarke and Gross, 2019) that teaching of social and emotional skills needs to be explicit, but also backed up by the wider classroom and school environment.

> *If we teach them [children] to communicate their feelings, they need adults out there in their everyday lessons who are prepared to listen to and respect those feelings. If we teach them not to lose control when they are angry, they need to see adults around them doing the same in school. If we teach them ways of resolving conflict, they need adults in the playground who can help them use their new skills.*

(Jean Gross, 2011)

As part of our intervention, a key target was to give pupils the language they needed to talk about different emotions. We decided to use a range of high-quality texts to support learning. According to Laurie Harper (2016), 'Picture books can provide the framework for building empathy, tolerance, and reinforce social-emotional, problem-solving, and conflict resolution skills in young children.'

Reading books and discussing illustrations was useful for helping children to develop their awareness of emotions. It also encouraged empathy by providing children in the class with the language to express, recognise and label emotions in themselves and others.

We were also influenced by our reading about anxiety: 'It's important for adults to normalise anxiety with children. It is simply a process of listening and creating a safe space for the young person to release the anxious thoughts and feelings weighing them down' (Harvey, 2021).

We wanted the children in the class to recognise that the negative emotions that they may feel are completely normal, acceptable and experienced by most of their peers. If children were aware that others have the same worries as they do, they might feel more comfortable to open up.

We wanted emotions to become part of daily classroom and playground conversations. Alongside the lessons that were to be delivered, our aim was for ad hoc discussions around emotions to become commonplace, with the class teachers finding opportunities to apply what the children had been learning to everyday classroom situations.

What we did

To lay the ground for new approaches in class, we needed to work with our colleagues in school. First, we shared our vision with the Leadership Team, who helped make it possible for teaching time on emotions to be prioritised in the timetable. We worked with the school's Behaviour Lead and Relationships and Health Lead, to ensure that introducing a new approach would be in line with current school policies and priorities, and worked with Year 3 staff to get them on board with the new approach.

We then implemented a series of lessons where children explored the range of emotions they feel and expanded the vocabulary they used to describe different emotions (Figure 6.2). We used circle time, books, drama, role play and scenario cards to support discussions.

Resources the children liked included the well-known 'Blob tree', where children identified which of a series of 'blob' figures best matched their current state of mind, and sentence starters to scaffold their ability to communicate how they were feeling (Figure 6.3).

Engagement in all these lessons was high although a challenge we encountered was the inability of children to think of real-life examples of more negative emotions and how to recognise these when they occur in their own class.

As part of the series of lessons, many scenarios were explored so that a range of emotions, both positive and negative, could be discussed. It was

Happy	Excited	Scared	Angry	Sad
Satisfied	Energetic	Tense	Upset	Blue
Content	Nervous	Jittery	Furious	Down
Fulfilled	Ecstatic	Anxious	Irritated	Mopey
Pleased	Bouncy	Terrified	Frustrated	Depressed
Serene	Animated	Fearful	Annoyed	Distracted
Elated	Distracted	Nervous	Resentful	Regretful
Joyful	Interested	Apprehensive	Bored	Grief-stricken

Figure 6.2   Expanding our emotional vocabulary

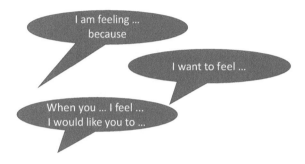

Figure 6.3   Sentence starters

important for the pupils to develop a clear understanding of more complex emotions such as guilt, frustration and resentment.

Introducing the Zones

Only when we had worked on emotion recognition and vocabulary were we able to begin to introduce our Zones of Regulation chart into the classroom. We read stories with SEMH themes and the class spoke about what Zones they recognised and which strategies the character(s) used to get out of the uncomfortable Zones. The children were easily able to link the emotions to the Zones and were aware that an emotional response to a situation differs from person to person.

Finally, a Zones of Regulation chart was put up in class and children were able to move their face to the appropriate zone. There is now time regularly devoted to speaking about which Zone they're in and why (sometimes using a script).

Children have responded well to the chart and have gradually become more willing to describe difficult feelings they and others are experiencing. It has been helpful that the Year 3 class we chose to focus on has two additional support staff who are on board with the project and its aims. When pupils need support and the class teacher is not available, these adults have provided opportunities for pupils to express their feelings. Every child is able to feel 'heard', even during busy times.

Support staff in the classroom have used the Zones as a way to prompt a child to communicate. For example, if a child is unresponsive but clearly upset, support staff would guide them to the Zones chart to move their picture.

What has come to light over this project is how long children hold on to emotions, even after the event. If they were hit by a ball at break time, for example, they would automatically put themselves in the Blue Zone even if the pain of the incident had gone away.

What we observed

The majority of our evidence comes from anecdotal feedback and video interviews completed with the children towards the end of the project, which demonstrated significant change.

What we observed was that children seemed to be very engaged with the Zones. For example, an incredibly shy child approached us on more than one occasion to tell us the Zone she was in and what made her feel that way. On another occasion, after a particularly inspiring phonics additionality group (delivered in a small group outside the classroom), a child came happily bounding back into the room and immediately moved his photo to the Green Zone to show his excitement and enthusiasm.

When interviewed, the children could use a greater range of vocabulary to describe different emotions and almost all children were able to articulate the purpose of using the Zones of Regulation. One child commented: 'The teachers need to know what we feel like, because if we feel sad, then they can help us and if we feel angry. But it's okay to feel those emotions.' When asked about the reason we talk about our emotions, another child said: 'If you talk about your emotions … you might feel better.'

In particular, those focus children who were reluctant to share their feelings, worries or anxieties at the beginning of the project had become able to communicate in a safe way, free from judgement.

Classroom climate also improved, with children more able to show empathy and support each other.

> I've noticed that children can get themselves out of a negative mood more easily. Children in the class try to help others to get into a better Zone and they try to cheer each other up.

(Miss H – Year 3 TA)

Through pupil interviews and observations by the class teacher and support staff, we can see that children are now more able to maintain focus on learning. None of the children in our focus group have made less-than-expected progress in all subjects across the year.

One interesting finding was that teachers report that they are now more likely to feed back to parents about how a child's day has been. They have also been able to share positives about the child.

> *Because of the success some children had with using the Zones of Regulation, the class teacher was able to communicate to a select group of parents how their child had used the chart in class to identify their emotions. The parents that were spoken to were receptive and proud of this information and encouraged these continued behaviours from their child.*

In the future, when we roll out the Zones school-wide, we aim to communicate with parents the practices happening in classrooms, with the hope that they could use some of the strategies, vocabulary and scripts at home.

Reflections

We are encouraged by the changes we have seen in this Year 3 class but cannot claim that it was only our project that led to this. Also important was our whole-school focus on restorative practice to resolve issues and conflicts with others. It is likely that the use of restorative practice techniques, the introduction of the Zones of Regulation and emotional literacy lessons all complemented each other, to lead to better pupil outcomes.

Another reflection point was that when using the Zones, children sometimes seemed to feel that the onus was on the teacher to 'help' or 'cheer up' the child. Moving forward, we'd like to see the children always use the strategies discussed in class themselves to get out of the uncomfortable Zones independently.

What we have learned

Through this project, we have had a positive and insightful experience of supporting and developing children's emotional literacy and vocabulary. Having tried similar interventions in the past and failing to embed these new initiatives, it is clear that investing time in the implementation of a new approach is key. Time is needed to support teaching staff and pupils to understand the purpose and process of the changes being made.

Our initial time spent on data collection and gathering qualitative pupil voice perspectives was invaluable in identifying what pupils needed. What we had first assumed would be a good research question didn't equate to what our pupils were telling us, so it was important to be flexible in our approach.

It was important, we learned, to dedicate a significant amount of curriculum time to explicitly teaching children emotional vocabulary. This was paramount before introducing the Zones of Regulation to create a culture of children feeling safe to share emotions and develop their knowledge of how to look after their mental health.

We have learned that there should be a clear progression in how emotional literacy is developed over the key stages. Our previous approach (the Colour Monster check-in) was a 'one-size fits all' activity and didn't allow for these tricky skills – such as self-awareness, regulation and management of your feelings – to evolve and grow as children moved through the school.

It was important to communicate our aims to our school leadership team and work closely with other senior members of staff such as our Behaviour Lead and Relationships and Health Lead to ensure that our priorities were aligned.

If we repeated this project, we would spend more time engaging our parents in the initiative and its desired outcomes so they had a better understanding of why a particular class was focusing on emotional literacy. It would also be useful for parents to continue discussions around emotions at home to support the learning being undertaken in school.

Finally, we have learned that it is important to begin a project like this on a small scale to ensure that it is successful before rolling it out to a whole-school approach. Having influential people (the 'innovator' and 'early adopter' types) involved as we roll out changes in the next academic year will ensure that our project is well-received. We can then move on to professional learning and organisational support and change to ensure the success of our initiative.

Next steps

Our next step is to use what we have learned from this intervention to roll out a Zones of Regulation approach in each classroom. Staff training will be important to ensure that all members of the teaching team are on board with this new initiative. This training will be carried out in conjunction with our Behaviour Lead and linked to staff training on restorative approaches, to ensure that there is consistency across the school and between different year groups.

It will also be important for us to be clear about the progression of vocabulary that we are teaching in KS1 and KS2 so that the language used in lessons is age-appropriate. Working alongside the Relationships and Health subject lead will be essential so that there is consistency within this scheme of work.

Finally, monitoring the rollout of this new approach will be important to ensure that all staff members are implementing the changes and to identify any issues that may arise in different year groups. We plan to do this through ongoing staff training, regular feedback sessions and discussions with teacher and pupil focus groups. Staying up to date with current research around emotional literacy will also be important for adapting our practice over time.

Key takeaways

- Work towards an approach to social and emotional learning that is used consistently across different age groups, as the skills of emotional literacy take time to develop.
- Plan for a progression in learning as children move up through the school, for example in the vocabulary for emotions that will be taught.
- Involve parents from the start, so that they can support children's learning at home.
- Help children understand that they have the power to regulate their own emotions and behaviour, rather than having to rely on the adults around them.

7 How we created calmer classrooms at Redriff Primary

Claire Taylor and Maia Mitchell

The children

We chose to focus our project on Year 4 pupils in the hope of developing more engagement with their overall learning, to create a calmer classroom environment and a reduction in the number of times teachers had to manage challenging behaviour.

Year 4 were selected because the co-author of this research project was a class teacher in that year group, but also as we had seen a few instances of classroom disruption, especially after key transitions, and wanted to find the most effective way to manage this. Across the year, the teachers had reported a (proportionally) high number of children who presented insecurities around learning and difficulties in managing and regulating stronger emotions.

Children at our school come from mixed backgrounds in terms of family size and circumstances, with some being specifically identified as not having as many opportunities to develop their emotional literacy in their home environment. Without input from school, many of these pupils would have very few opportunities to discuss emotions or develop their emotional literacy – a focus for our PSHE and Oracy curriculum across the school.

We hoped starting with Year 4 as a baseline, regular routine calm time and explicit teaching of SEL skills would be something we could roll out across the school in the next academic year.

Gathering information

At the start and end of our project we used an ImpactEd Wellbeing Questionnaire to measure children's wellbeing. We also developed a questionnaire for adults to gather qualitative data about the current classroom climate, barriers to a calm classroom and how the climate could be improved.

We were seeking the views of both pupils and teachers to help us decide on the aspects of emotional wellbeing within the classroom that could become the focus of the specific SEL skills teaching throughout the project. Teachers reported disrupted playtimes due to a perceived lack of support with disagreements in play and challenges managing unregulated children in an already busy timetabled day.

DOI: 10.4324/9781003396796-7

What we learned from research and wider reading

From research on mindfulness in schools (see for example https://mindful nessinschools.org/research-papers/), the work of expert Adele Bates (Bates, 2021), and the EEF's guidance report on improving social and emotional learning in primary schools (Van Poortvliet, Clarke and Gross, 2019) we learned that there is a known impact on pupils' outcomes and learning behaviours when they are able to successfully self-regulate. This is achieved best when there is peer-on peer-influence and recognition from peers as well as from adults.

What we did

We started by making changes in just one of the Year 4 classes, beginning with regular mindfulness breathing after transitional times (the start and end of the school day, and after play times). We did this as we had identified these times to be particularly unsettled, with a larger number of disagreements and unregulated behaviours.

The breathing exercises were taken from the Anna Freud Centre's Mindfulness Calendar (https://mentallyhealthyschools.org.uk/resources/ mindfulness-calendar-daily-five-minute-activities/), which includes everything from 'birthday cake breathing' to 'feather breathing' and 'slimy hand..' After we had tried out the different ideas, children could then choose those that most resonated with them, when they needed to feel calmer.

The pupils' responses to the ImpactEd wellbeing measure showed us that a large proportion of children in our focus class felt they were 'more than often' dealing with strong emotions (this was specified as sadness, frustration but also anxiety or concern). We used the data in the form of heat mapping, which allowed us to see clearly who was in the amber or the red areas for their overall wellbeing.

We then used the heat mapping data to re-evaluate how pupils' positioning on the carpet and partners for talk were potentially affecting their wellbeing, finding that those on the outside of the carpet space were experiencing higher levels of anxiety. We moved these children so that they were more central, hoping that this would support their emotional wellbeing by making them feel more involved in the class.

In addition, we established pupil wellbeing ambassadors as additional support during playtimes. They were tasked with giving advice to others if a disagreement occurred, modelling good practice of self-regulation and ensuring that no child was left vulnerable during these times.

Following the EEF guidance, all adults involved were encouraged to model positive self-talk and self-calming strategies for the pupils to mirror. We particularly noticed that when adults named their emotions and labelled their own coping strategies, the pupils, in turn, began to do this more often.

> When I identified times when I was struggling emotionally, labelled it and said out loud what strategy I would use, I noticed pupils doing this with each other.

(**Y4 teacher**)

The 'taught' curriculum

Alongside teacher modelling, we established protected time for a weekly SEL skill session, using role-play to show two sides to situations and create an opportunity for self-reflection, as well as opportunities for problem-solving in pairs/small groups. It was challenging at first to find the balance between teaching time and discussion time, as the time slot was relatively short, but as the sessions continued, the discussions flowed more easily and it became a more natural process of dividing time between taught time and open problem-solving time.

One of our SEL lessons was about how our brains work, looking at the different areas of the brain and the 'brain house' metaphor, using the BBC video www.bbc.co.uk/teach/class-clips-video/pshe-ks2-the-brain-house/zd7kd6f and Dan Siegel's model of the brain 'flipping its lid' when feelings take over and we can no longer think sensibly.

In other lessons we worked on words for feelings, drawing on Plutchik's 'wheel of emotions.' There are many versions of the wheel on the internet, and a very useful interactive version at www.6seconds.org/2022/03/13/plutchik-wheel-emotions/.

In the wheel's centre are the words mad, scared, sad, joyful, powerful and peaceful. Each of these are 'unpacked' into related words in outer circles.

To start with, we asked children to look at just the centre of the wheel. We asked whether these were the only words to describe our emotions, and invited children to add to the wheel on a flipchart. Later they looked at the full wheel and were asked to identify words that were new and interesting. Finally, they had a 'talk task' (Figure 7.1), in which they had to discuss where to place words within the basic sad/mad/scared /joyful powerful/peaceful categories.

Another lesson looked at the words associated with resilience, or lack of it (Figures 7.2 and 7.3).

Talk task: Can you match the emotions together?

inferior	sad
sceptical	mad
pensive	scared
valuable	joyful
optimistic	powerful
inadequate	peaceful

Figure 7.1   Talk task

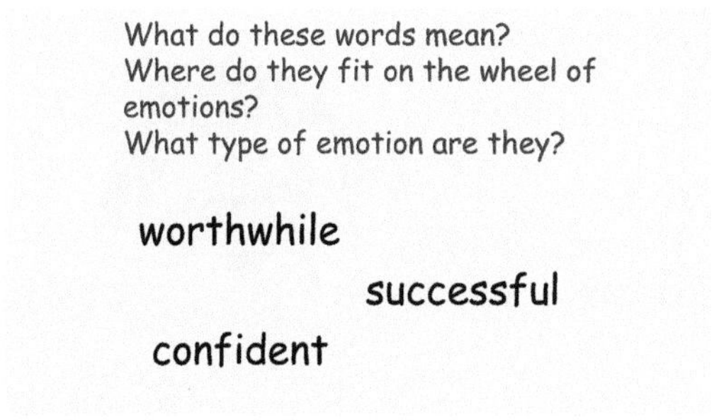

What do these words mean?
Where do they fit on the wheel of emotions?
What type of emotion are they?

worthwhile

successful

confident

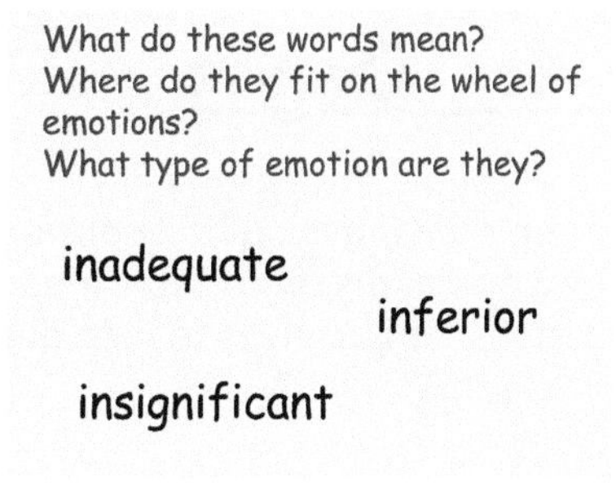

What do these words mean?
Where do they fit on the wheel of emotions?
What type of emotion are they?

inadequate

inferior

insignificant

Figures 7.2 and 7.3   Resilience task

Children were asked to talk to a partner about how they would know if someone was resilient, and come up with an example of a time when they themselves showed resilience. Finally, the class discussed why we need resilience and what we could do to become more resilient. 'Should we add resilience to our class charter?', they were asked, and 'Will you all sign it?'

Looking at another type of social and emotional skill – relationships – we also worked on kindness. We asked children to draw and talk to a partner about a time when someone was kind to them, and how they felt. They drew round their hands and labelled each finger with a different way of showing kindness. After break and lunchtime they reported back on acts of kindness they had seen. We thought about how to be kind in what we say to other. We squeezed a tube of toothpaste and asked the children if it was possible to put the toothpaste back in the tube; they discussed how unkind words are a bit like that – they can't be 'unsaid', and they can make others feel sad.

A whole-school vision

Research suggests that having a shared vision in order to create a whole-school culture is key to a prolonged realisation of a project. Using a whole-staff meeting, we were able to introduce the project and promote some elements of it as a whole-school focus during Place2Be's 2022 Children's Mental Health and Wellbeing Week. We planned lessons on the science of the brain for other teachers to deliver, an assembly and a whole-school display, providing templates for colleagues to use to share their work (Figures 7.4 and 7.5).

This in turn gave opportunities for a wider network of people within the school to share their own experiences of mindfulness and teaching social and emotional skills. From this sharing opportunity, we were able to adapt the project within Year 4, so it remained relevant and a continued success.

Key people in our wider network were the pastoral team, who helped us with valuable ideas of websites to use and organisations to look into that they often use as a reference for their small-group interventions. We worked with these ideas to create something that could work in a larger, whole-class setting.

Year 4 – Danae

We have been thinking about how our brain works. Sometimes we have uncomfortable feelings. We can say 'affirmations' to ourselves to help our brain stay calm and focused.

Danae drew a picture of herself and then wrote some messages that she could read herself if she started to feel sad or angry.

Danae wrote 'I can do anything', 'I am kind' and 'I am brave.'

Figure 7.4   Y4 work shared at an assembly

In Year 2 , we started our week by singing Reach for The Stars by S Club 7. We set ourselves goals we would like to achieve and thought about what steps we need to take to achieve these.

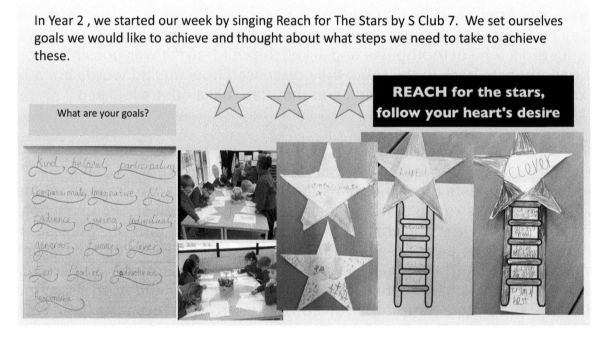

Figure 7.5   Y2 work shared at an assembly

Impact

Using data from the ImpactEd wellbeing assessment with the pupils (Figure 7.6), we were able to see a 3.63% increase on average in how the pupils perceived their wellbeing, as well as their feelings of confidence and contentment in their class setting.

Wellbeing [BASELINE]	Wellbeing [FINAL]
2.14	3
3.14	1.57
3.29	4.14
3.71	4
3.71	3.86
4.14	2.29
3.29	4.14
2.71	2.71
3.57	3.14
4.57	3.57
3.57	3.86
3.71	4.57
3.57	4.14
3.57	3.71
3.43	3.86
2.71	3.43
3.57	4.57
3.71	3
3.57	4

Figure 7.6   Wellbeing scores

The greatest impact was on boys, who showed a 4.67% increase in wellbeing scores, compared to a 2.79% increase amongst girls. This is of particular interest as we found the boys were (in general) harder to engage in discussions around their emotions and found it more challenging to learn specific new SEL skills.

Although we saw a higher increase in wellbeing amongst the boys in the year group, we were cautious about attributing this finding to the work of our project. We wondered whether the data might be skewed by the boys' own initial perceptions or misconceptions about wellbeing, and by how they judged their own wellbeing. The baseline data showed children who were known to struggle to deal with stronger emotions and required a lot of support with regulation had perceived themselves as happy in school and that they dealt with strong feelings 'little or none of the time.' By the end of the project, their self-perceptions may have become more realistic, perhaps because our explicit SEL teaching made them more self-aware.

To ensure our findings were as accurate as possible, we interviewed some key children and asked them to explain elements of their emotional literacy learning. It was interesting to observe that all were more confident to talk about specific strategies than they were at the beginning of the project. This, together with visually seeing a difference in their learning behaviours and coping mechanisms, led us to measure the success of the project as moderate to high.

The children who showed the greatest gains in wellbeing were the two we had asked to be wellbeing ambassadors, supporting other children in the playground. These children had a 21% and 19% increase in their own perception of wellbeing. We wondered if that might be because becoming ambassadors allowed them to make accelerated progress in their own understanding of SEL, and also developed their sense of self-efficacy.

What we learned

We have learned that through a whole-class approach to teaching SEL skills, including skills of empathy, being a good friend, handling conflict and being resilient, pupils were able to support their peers. This supports Jean Gross' argument in Chapter 1 of this book, that SEL work has the greatest impact by targeting all pupils rather than only small groups of children with the highest need, creating a classroom environment and culture where children with SEMH needs will be supported by their peers. All children were able to benefit and grow emotionally. Explicitly teaching self-regulation enabled them to identify emotions in each other. This has meant that they can support each other with strategies to self-regulate.

We also learned that teaching mindfulness strategies when not in 'crisis mode' allows the strategies to be embedded and become more effective when those 'crisis points' occur. Teachers said that incidents in managing behaviour had decreased due to a refocus after playtimes on establishing a calm classroom environment. The specific mindfulness breathing activities were commented on in particular as being a great refocus for the whole class. In interviews, teachers also noted that explicitly teaching strategies for self-regulation had a big impact on the number of disagreements or challenges they had to manage after playtimes.

Finally, we learned that research is a powerful professional development tool, which we as a school could use more widely.

> As a school, we are currently taking a more structured approach to our staff meetings by including an element of research in each. Every relevant staff meeting, the teachers are divided into groups and given or chosen a specific piece of research, that is then fed back to the whole group.

(Senior Leadership Team member)

Working with parents

Our parents were supportive of and complementary about the focus on emotions, with one parent commenting on their child teaching them some mindfulness breathing activities to try together at home, and another parent adding that their child often came home with a new 'emotion buzz word' that they wanted to share with the family.

Further to this project, we would like to continue involving parents, but hopefully on a larger scale, for example running some parent workshops alongside the pastoral team to continue our work on specific teaching of SEL skills and mindfulness activities that can be used in their home environment.

Key takeaways

- Explicit teaching of SEL works best when adults name emotions and create time to explain them clearly, modelling ways of managing feelings for the children to see.
- It helps to start innovations small-scale, to allow for refinements and to take the time for challenges to be addressed before rolling out change more widely across the school.
- Providing colleagues with pre-prepared activities (for example, mindfulness activities) and SEL skills sessions that can be used and adapted for different year groups helps ensure buy-in.
- It is useful to draw on a variety of evidence to assess pupils' wellbeing, including data from teachers as well as from pupils, and anecdotal evidence.
- Linking a member of SLT to innovations tested by an individual teacher is essential, so that the lead teacher is well supported, and the project will fit with the whole school development plan and SEMH strategy.
- It is important to allow any teacher assigned to lead SEL developments adequate time to research and compile ideas initially, and then present their findings to the rest of the year group team and secure wider buy-in for the project

8 How we involved children in an initiative to tackle football problems at lunch and breaktimes at Shaftesbury Primary

Zainab Khonat, Joanne O'Connor and Aaron Bennett

The children

Our project focused on a group of boys in Year 4 who had struggled to manage their emotions and behaviours when playing football, basketball and cricket during school breaktimes. Observations of these boys and scrutiny of the behaviour records held in school confirmed that these pupils were involved in numerous recorded behaviour incidents ranging from low to moderate levels of disruption. We noticed that they struggled to play in a co-operative way and there were many emotional outbursts and challenging behaviours. Pupils' negative behaviour was consuming far too much valuable learning time, as disputes would be brought into the classroom on a daily basis.

What we learned from research

We were interested to read how important explicit lessons are for the teaching of social and emotional literacy and that such lessons can be applied in many different curriculum areas (Gross, 2022). In line with Bates' (2021) advice, we felt that what we were seeing in these pupils' behaviour was the communication of an unmet need, and that if we did not understand this fully we would be reacting to the behaviour instead of addressing the underlying issue long term. We also drew on the work of Desautels (2019) who said that when teachers listen to what is beneath a behaviour, the child will view this as being 'seen' and know that the teacher is trying to understand, instead of to punish.

Gathering baseline data

As a result of our reading, we spent time observing the pupils at play and had informal conversations with them to try and identify what the issues

DOI: 10.4324/9781003396796-8

were. We saw and heard that too many pupils would try to take control of the game; when there were too many voices and opinions, arguments became harder to resolve. Pupils admitted that they did not actually know the rules, and this uncertainty created conflict. Finally, they did not see playing outdoor games as a team-building activity but rather as a place of competition where they were trying to dominate and 'win', even against their own teammates.

Changes to teaching and learning

We began a lunchtime support group with our sports coach each day (Figure 8.1). After lunch the group would meet him in the sports hall for a 30-minute session which concentrated on developing their skills for co-operative games.

The sports coach looked at rules and organisation of the three main games played outdoors but with a particular focus on football. The children agreed rules and procedures as well as unpicking what causes problems when the game is not refereed by an adult. They practised using their negotiating skills through games, discussed how best to resolve disputes, the importance of empathising with others' situations and how to play collaboratively.

Pupils came up with a charter that they all signed up to, and agreed on consequences such as a one-match ban for breaking the rules (Figure 8.2).

Figure 8.1   Coach Noah and the children

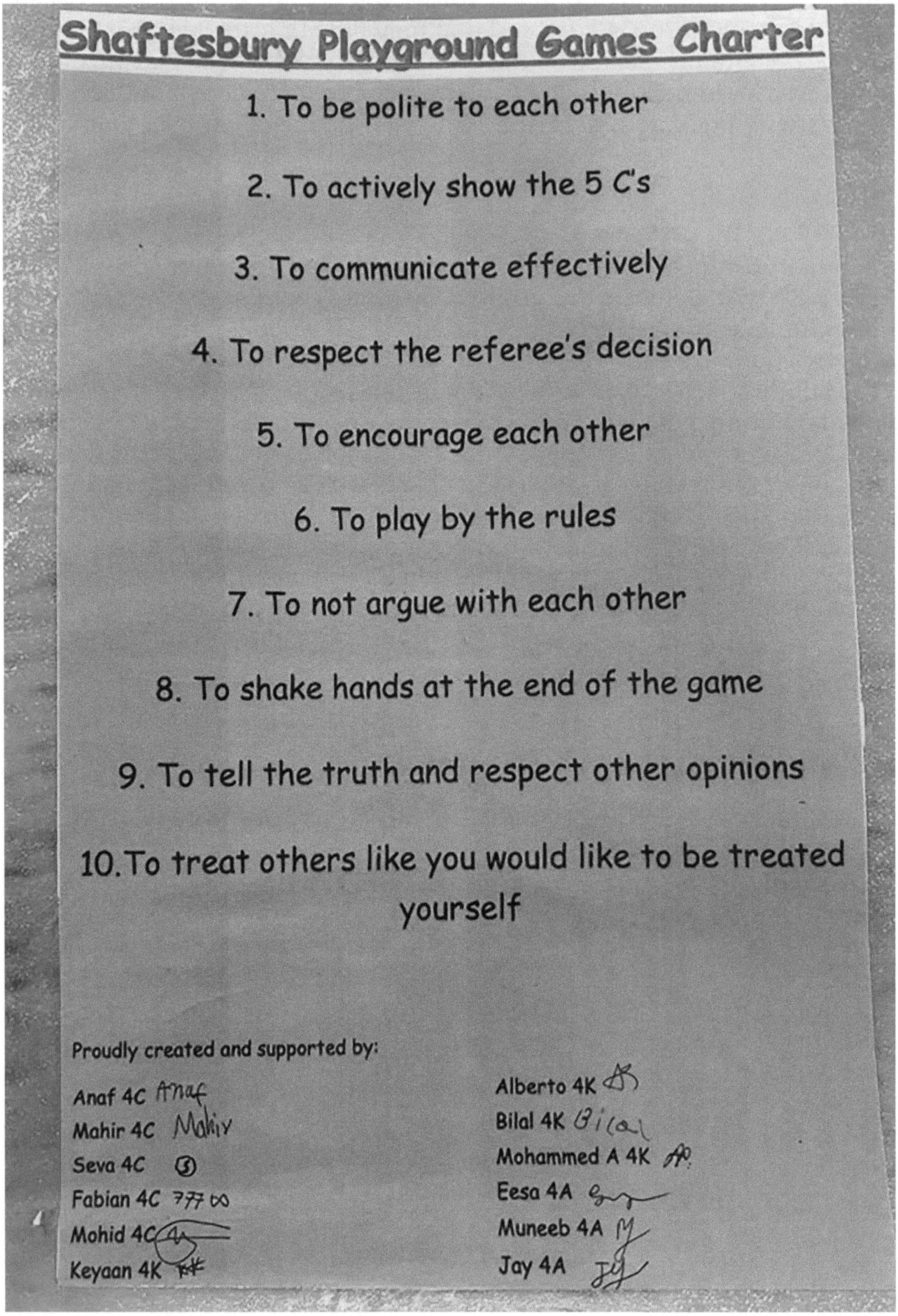

Shaftesbury Playground Games Charter

1. To be polite to each other

2. To actively show the 5 C's

3. To communicate effectively

4. To respect the referee's decision

5. To encourage each other

6. To play by the rules

7. To not argue with each other

8. To shake hands at the end of the game

9. To tell the truth and respect other opinions

10. To treat others like you would like to be treated yourself

Proudly created and supported by:

Anaf 4C *Anaf*
Mahir 4C *Mahir*
Seva 4C *(S)*
Fabian 4C *777 ∞*
Mohid 4C *signature*
Keyaan 4K *signature*

Alberto 4K *signature*
Bilal 4K *Bilal*
Mohammed A 4K *signature*
Eesa 4A *signature*
Muneeb 4A *M signature*
Jay 4A *signature*

Figure 8.2   The playground charter

These indoor sessions took place over a period of eight weeks and then continued outdoors, where the boys received gradually less input from the coach and lighter-touch supervision.

The impact

Once the eight-week programme had ended, pupils began to play outside again more independently. We observed that there was a better understanding around large group games, how to organise and play fairly.

Behaviour tracking showed that there were fewer disruptions and disagreement, meaning less incidents to investigate once back in the classroom and teachers have reported that less learning time is lost. Teachers also noted that productive playtimes and lunchtimes meant pupils were more easily able to focus once they were back in class, which did improve the quality and quantity of work they produced. Pupils were able to resolve disputes themselves and take actions to repair relationships (Figure 8.3).

An analysis of our behaviour tracker revealed that these pupils have been awarded a higher number of 'green points' for various different reasons, for example behaviour, participation in discussion, answering questions, work outcomes. Our project mainly focused on improving relationships and behaviour but there has definitely been progress in academic achievement (Figure 8.4).

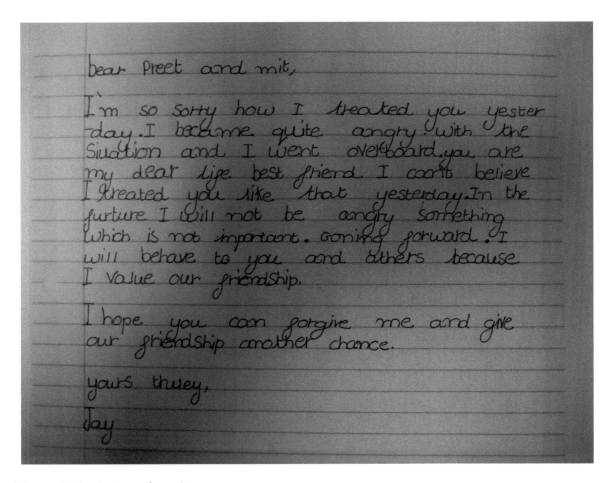

Figure 8.3   Letter of apology

Figure 8.4   Receiving a 'green point'

As part of the school's partnership work to resolve issues and support learning, parents are often included in managing behaviour, but this is unfortunately often focused on negative events. However, during the project all staff including class teachers, students, PE coach, learning mentor, midday supervisors, behaviour lead and teaching assistants were able to focus on the 'catch them being good' strategy (Figure 8.5). Parents received much more positive feedback in terms of postcards sent home electronically and they have told us that this has helped their interactions with their own children out of school. Rather than trying to unpick why something has happened, they have been able to celebrate an achievement with their child.

What next at Shaftesbury?

As a result of the project, the senior leadership team discussed the wider PE curriculum, in particular the fact that we cannot automatically assume that pupils know how to play in larger groups with each other co-operatively and that this has to be taught explicitly. We decided to adapt the current

Figure 8.5   Celebrating great behaviour

curriculum so that instead of teaching games in the summer term, there is some earlier teaching to enable pupils to understand the rules from the start of the year.

In order to achieve this, the PE, behaviour and PSHE leaders constructed units of work that will enable pupils to learn how to organise and manage group games, in the hope that these additional skills will equip children to negotiate and facilitate more successful group games during independent time in the playground. A typical six-week unit of work includes two to four sessions on co-operative games that will be taught at the start of each term, and include both indoor and outdoor games.

We also provided all pupils across the school with team-building activities and football skills sessions. This included children refereeing and organising their own football games.

Since the COVID lockdown, we have realised that many of our pupils are still struggling to express their own emotions and behaviours. To this end, and as a result of hearing from other schools on this project, we are going to implement the regular use of the Zones of Regulation from Nursery to Year 6. We hope that in this way, the project will have a lasting impact on the learning and enjoyment of PE, and on the wellbeing of pupils across the school.

Reflections

For myself, I have learnt that you need to be pro-active about supporting pupils with SEMH needs. Many are different but sometimes you can group pupils for support to meet some of these needs. It is not something that can be accomplished alone by the class teacher. Some pupils have long-term issues that have been ingrained for a long period of time and change for them doesn't happen quickly.

(Teacher)

The project has impacted the way we look at the teaching structure for next academic year. One of the classes with some of the pupil participants has undergone lots of change this year, with their class teacher leaving at Christmas and then a mix of other teachers put in to replace. We have chosen very carefully the teachers that our Year 4 cohort will have next year to try and ensure consistency and quality of provision. If we had not identified this group and looked in more depth at issues they were experiencing we might not have considered this as much as we have.

(Leader)

Key takeaways

- Never assume that pupils know how to play positively together.
- Skills for collaborative play need to be taught and built into the curriculum, even though they may not be clearly identified within the National Curriculum objectives.
- Providing play equipment for pupils is not enough; schools also need to devote time to showing pupils how to use the equipment provided and to explaining how to organise larger group games.
- Pupils may love playing football and other such ball games, but the skills and the rules need to be taught if they are to play fairly and to include others.

9 How we engaged children with learning at Portway Primary and Pinner Primary

Saidat Olajide and Casey Rich, Portway Primary
Sarah Marriott and Emily Thomas,
Pinner Wood Primary

The children

Both Pinner Wood and Portway identified that a particular cohort had difficulty regulating their emotions, which in turn had a detrimental effect on their behaviour and their learning.

At Pinner Wood, we felt that Year 5 struggled with the ability to express their own feelings and to understand how this affected their behaviour. Many children were spending time with learning mentors, looking to these adults to solve their problems. We used a wellbeing survey in December 2021 and this revealed that tiredness and headaches were an issue for this cohort but that they were generally a happy group of pupils, at the 68th centile (still in the average range). We also did some low-level behaviour incident tracking, whereby the team monitored and tallied each time the children were spoken to because of their behaviour, over the course of a day. This tally revealed that some children received a high number of reminders and teacher inputs to help them behave appropriately. These same children were presenting low levels of engagement, as evidenced through our use of the Leuven Scale, the average score for involvement being 2.91 and the average for wellbeing 2.95.

Year 2 children at Portway presented as being emotionally immature for their age and having particular difficulty expressing and regulating emotions. This seemed to have a negative impact on both behaviour, including regular low-level disruption, and engagement in learning. The children also had a limited language for expressing their emotions, often using a basic vocabulary, for example sad, mad, happy or angry. The Year 2 cohort was identified as being one of the year groups that was most impacted by the pandemic, with some of them never having had an uninterrupted year of school.

The focus children chosen within the year group, while not necessarily behind academically, were not achieving their potential due to their difficulties with emotional regulation. Our initial observations of the focus children revealed lower than average Leuven Scale scores for both involvement and

DOI: 10.4324/9781003396796-9

wellbeing compared to their peers. Across Year 2, the Leuven baseline scores showed that approximately half the students had moderate to low scores for wellbeing and involvement. For involvement, 44% of students showed on average a moderate level, and though engaged in mainly continuous activity, children were at a fairly routine level of involvement with few signs of genuine engagement. They would make some progress with their learning but not show a lot of energy or concentration. Many were also often easily distracted: 6% of children showed low levels of involvement, with frequently interrupted activity and moments of non-activity when distracted. In terms of wellbeing, 36% of students were found to have on average a moderate to low level, ranging from signs of discomfort or unease to becoming visibly distressed and crying.

Work samples at Portway showed inconsistency of engagement, with key children often producing a lower quantity and quality of work than class teachers knew them to be capable of. When work samples were cross-referenced with attainment data, it was clear that there was a divide between students' abilities and the work they were producing day-to-day.

What we learned from the research

We were interested to read that social, emotional and mental health needs are becoming more and more prominent within schools and that behavioural and emotional difficulties can have long-term consequences (Gross, 2022). Chowdry and McBride (2017) have found that such problems at age five contribute to emotional and behavioural problems at age ten, and to lower cognitive scores (on maths and reading tests) at age ten, which in turn contribute to lower cognitive scores at age 16 (on arithmetic and vocabulary tests). It is crucial, then, for primary schools to put in place the right support for students as early as possible.

From research, we learned that teachers need to consider their own self-regulation in order to understand and influence pupils (Bates, 2022) since the teacher is a model for the children in their class. Teachers need to model the thought process behind self-regulation at the children's level as this is how to teach children about regulation and to help them better understand emotions and feelings. Bates (2022) also discusses the risk that if adults are not regulated there is the potential for the children to feel increased anxiety and stress which is more likely to evoke behavioural outbursts.

Similarly, we learned that as teachers we need to teach self-regulation explicitly. This is supported by EEF guidance (Van Poortvliet, Clarke and Gross, 2019), which stresses the importance of using metacognition and self-regulation strategies for collaborative groups so that learners can support each other and make their thinking explicit through discussion. Kuypers (2011) advises teachers to teach scaffolded skills in order to develop a metacognitive pathway which can help pupils recognise their own emotions and develop a set of tools and strategies for self-regulation, relationship building and wellbeing. Desautels' (2019) work revealed that it is important to validate children's feelings in order to establish a safe space in which the children can discuss how feelings affect choices and consequences for their behaviour.

What we did

At both Portway and Pinner Wood, we hoped that explicitly teaching emotional vocabulary would equip the students to articulate their feelings as well as begin to choose strategies to self-regulate (Figure 9.1). This would in turn positively impact their ability to focus in lessons. Both schools decided that the Zones of Regulation tool would be the best approach to focus on as it would give the children the strategies and language to identify and manage their emotions.

At Portway, we began by introducing the Colour Monster story to the whole school as a starting point for talking about emotions. We then introduced and worked hard to embed the Zones of Regulation to equip students with language to identify their feelings as well as begin to choose strategies for emotional regulation. While the Zones of Regulation work well as a whole school system to support behaviour, we have found that it is not enough on its own to support children who struggle to self-regulate. Within this context, and based on our learning from the literature, we decided to do some additional explicit teaching of emotional vocabulary.

Class teachers began by assessing the level of vocabulary children already had around the different emotions, using the Zones of Regulation as a starting point. Teachers then built in time weekly to explicitly teach emotion vocabulary. Learning from these sessions was displayed in the classroom so it could be referred to throughout the school day (Figure 9.2).

The feelings check-in used with students during registration each day (Figure 9.3) was adapted to reflect a wider emotional vocabulary (Figure 9.4). This allowed teachers to have a clearer idea of how each student was feeling each morning and afternoon and allowed them to identify any children needing further support. Class teachers regularly modelled naming their own feelings and choosing strategies to regulate themselves. This helped to normalise talking about feelings for the children and help them to feel safe and confident to try it themselves.

At Pinner Wood, we decided to introduce the Zones of Regulation through four discrete lessons, tackling one Zone per lesson. Teachers used

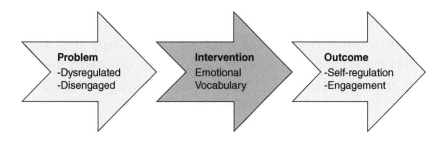

Figure 9.1   Our hypothesis

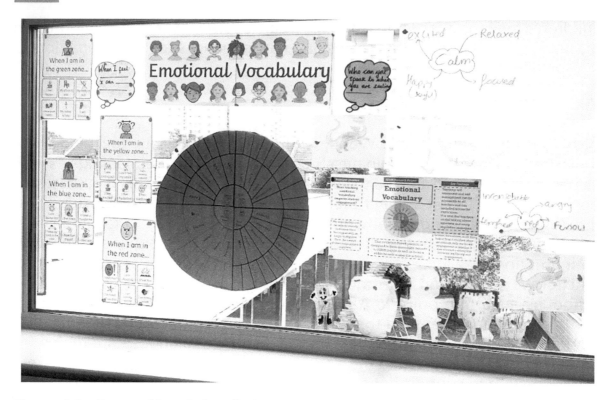

Figure 9.2   Zones of Regulation display

Figure 9.3   Display to support children to identify their emotions (Portway)

collaborative talk activities to reinforce the importance of sharing and cooperating with one another. At first, teachers were allowing the children to move their names from one Zone to another at any time. Teachers found that this was difficult to manage, however, so we introduced set times including morning check-ins, after break and after lunch, to add structure to the day. We noticed that these were the times when the children's emotions could be heightened and so focusing on these transitions gave us a clearer understanding of what was affecting emotional changes.

Another strategy we used was to create a calm corner where the children could go if they needed to calm down. At first, the children benefited from an adult sitting with them in this space, but over time they were able to regulate their feelings independently, without any adult support.

Figure 9.4   Display to support children to identify their emotions (Pinner Wood)

Like Portway, we did some explicit teaching about different emotions; how these present and can be identified and managed. We wanted the children to have a vocabulary to name emotions, strategies to recognise these in themselves, and the agency to act on this knowledge. The aim was for the children to not seek adult advice, but instead to have a bank of resources that they could access themselves, whenever they needed. One way we enabled this agency was by ensuring discussions were open and safe, and that children understood how important it was to support each other.

The impact

Both at Portway and Pinner Wood schools, we can honestly say we have seen some great progress in the children's learning behaviours, especially the key children we identified at the beginning of the project.

Portway

At Portway, teachers have reported big changes in the emotional language being used by the class in general. The children now have a wider emotional vocabulary and can talk in-depth about the emotions they are experiencing.

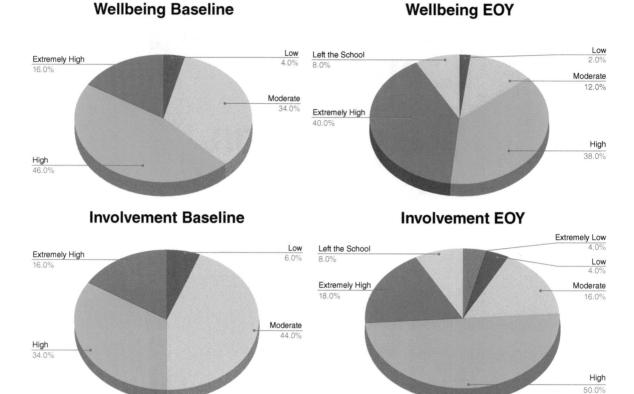

Figures 9.5 and 9.6   Graph of baseline-impact wellbeing data (Leuven Scale)

Children who previously displayed anxious behaviour have gained confidence and seem to be a lot happier in school generally and in terms of friendships. Teachers reported children being generally happier and more cheerful, and expressing self-confidence and self-assurance. By the end of the year (EOY), Leuven Scale scores corroborated this anecdotal evidence: only 16% of students showed a moderate level of involvement (which is reasonably low) compared to 42% before the intervention began, and only 12% of students showed on average a moderate to low level of wellbeing compared to 34% before the intervention (Figures 9.5 and 9.6). Possibly most rewardingly, students have commented on their own development and how they feel more able to focus on work and make expected choices as a result of the intervention

An analysis of work samples revealed an increase in both quantity and quality of work produced by children (Figure 9.7). All of the identified focus children made expected or above progress in their attainment, with three out of the five children making accelerated progress.

Focus child case studies: Portway

RR was on the verge of being excluded due to the number of instances of either repeated low-level disruption or physical incidents and was repeatedly involved in restorative conversations with staff and family. One of the main reasons this was happening, was that he lacked the

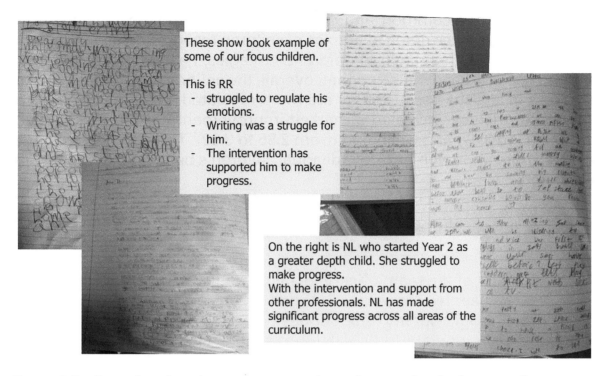

These show book example of some of our focus children.

This is RR
- struggled to regulate his emotions.
- Writing was a struggle for him.
- The intervention has supported him to make progress.

On the right is NL who started Year 2 as a greater depth child. She struggled to make progress.
With the intervention and support from other professionals. NL has made significant progress across all areas of the curriculum.

Figure 9.7   Examples of work samples pre- and post-intervention for focus pupils

ability to regulate his emotions and the confidence to express himself. RR received behaviour points in Autumn Term (the start of the project), two in the Spring Term and none in Summer Term. When we interviewed him, RR explained that he is now open to talking about his emotions and described the strategies he uses to help regulate himself when he is in the 'Red Zone.'

NE was a child who struggled with emotional regulation and this was having a significant impact on learning outcomes. Since the project began, as her Leuven Scores improved, the quality and quantity of the work in her books also improved.

Feedback from parents also suggested positive changes they had seen in their child's behaviour. We had a meeting with RN's mum, for example, who wanted to thank us teachers for the support he was receiving and was very pleased with how much he has grown and developed over just a few months.

Pinner Wood

At Pinner Wood, teachers found the project had a similar impact on both behaviour and learning. Teachers reported that the children were better able to name different emotions, to share ideas on how to 'get back to the Green

Zone' and shared a common language for discussing emotions. Observations of classroom practice noted examples of children recognising and managing their emotions with a range of different strategies. Feedback from teachers and the Pastoral Lead indicated that, overall, the children are making quicker progress in lessons because they are more regulated. Leuven Scale data at the end of the year revealed a marked improvement in both involvement (from 2.91 to 3.61) and wellbeing (from 2.95 to 3.92). There were also lots of stories about improvements to individual children's behaviour, learning and wellbeing.

Focus child case studies: Pinner Wood

One member of the team observed a vulnerable child, AA, saying: 'It's too loud so I am feeling terrified.' When asked what they could do, this child said 'I could put my headphones on.' His teacher noted that prior to the intervention, the child's default response to this situation would have been screaming and crying.

Child AB was seen to have become much more confident in moving her name on the Zones display after every lesson and better able to articulate how she was feeling. As a result, unlike in the Autumn Term when she was refusing to go into assembly or being told off during assembly, she was able to stay in the hall with minimum intervention.

TU was reported by his teacher to be much more articulate in describing how he was feeling and which Zone he was in, as well as giving reasons for why he felt that way, for example: 'I'm feeling in the yellow Zone because I'm scared of the rain outside, so can I stay inside please?' This example also reveals how he managed to find a solution independently and this meant that after break time he was better able to access learning in the classroom. The teacher contrasted this behaviour to previous similar situations where he would have been likely to catastrophise and may have needed to spend a considerable amount of time calming down.

Impact on parents

From anecdotal evidence, the project also had an impact on parents and carers at both schools. Child PQ's mum told teachers at Pinner Wood that she uses the language and techniques that have been taught in school, for example asking her child what Zone he is in and reminding him of regulation techniques like 'mountain breathing', 'going to your happy place' and '5, 4, 3, 2, 1.' At Portway, RN's mum came in to thank teachers for the support he was receiving and to let them know how pleased she was with how much he has matured and developed throughout the year.

Wider school impact and next steps

The project enabled Pinner Wood to influence a range of staff in different year groups. The most effective strategy for influencing was starting our regular morning staff briefings with a check-in using the Zones of Regulation. Modelling this with staff encouraged teachers to replicate this in their classrooms at the beginning of the day (Figure 9.8). One PGCE student, based in Early Years, decided to focus her teaching and learning research project on the benefits of using the Zones of Regulation to manage emotions and improve behaviour. Moving forward, we plan to conduct more in-depth training on the Zones of Regulation for all staff.

At Portway, we created a poster to share information about the project with all teachers and update them on its progress (Figure 9.9). Since the project ended, the Wellness Lead has been considering how best to begin to widen the impact of the project across the school, and initially plans to use elements of the intervention in the school's end-of-year transition period.

Figure 9.8   Zones of Regulation display (Pinner Wood)

Research Question	SEMH Research Project	Key Findings
Does teaching emotional vocabulary improve student engagement?	**Emotional Vocabulary**	- Teaching self awareness and self management can be accessible to all teachers and can included across the curriculum. - It is vital that teachers model talking about emotions and using regulation strategies.
We want students to be able to identify and name their feelings as well as begin to regulate them. As a result student engagement improves.	This evidence based project is designed to have immediate benefit to SEMH pupils as well as have a wider benefit across the school.	Leuven data shows more than half of Year 2 children show on average only moderate engagement in lessons. It also showed a strong link between wellbeing and engagement.

Figure 9.9   Project poster (Portway)

During transition days, classes will create their own emotional vocabulary displays which will then be available for them to refer and add to over the next academic year. We will also share the resources and information from the explicit teaching of emotional vocabulary used in the project so that class teachers can use and adapt this in their own classrooms.

As a result of anecdotal evidence of impact on families, both schools plan to run sessions with parents and carers in the coming academic year to share the techniques teachers have been using, so that parents and carers can also use them at home. At Portway, we also plan to design related homework tasks to be done as a family, including information packs with vocabulary lists families can use.

In addition, attitudes towards research as the basis for influencing approaches to teaching and learning across schools have become more positive. There is more of a focus on understanding the rationale for any changes to practice in terms of the evidence that supports it, and on putting research at the heart of everything we do.

Reflections

It has been possible to see first-hand the difference the project has made to their individual students and to their classroom as a whole. We have enjoyed this process and it has been a joy to see the changes in the children.

(Teacher, Portway)

I learnt that the teacher as the model is a very effective tool and teachers are able to model and instil the desired behaviour of learners. This is like a self-fulfilling prophecy …: the children were able to believe in the strategies they were adopting, on the basis the teacher was using them too.

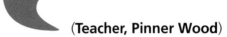

(Teacher, Pinner Wood)

It has been helpful to see how the project was able to be delivered, on a small scale, with minimal extra workload but with significant impact. I will be able to use the learning from this experience to influence the wider school community and recommend the intervention using the evidence gained through the project.

It has been extremely insightful to learn the steps of running a research project. In future, were we to identify a further area of investigation we would feel confident that we would be able to follow these same steps in another context. Being able to gather a range of data made it easy to evidence the changes that we saw in the children, so not only did we see improvement but we could prove it as well.

(Leader, Portway)

I learnt that it is important to start small before moving into a bigger project and this scaffolding has supported us in implementing this project across the school. I have learnt how to influence others by including central people in the decision making through the research about Adopter Types.

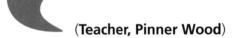

(Teacher, Pinner Wood)

Key takeaways

- The Zones of Regulation is a simple and practical approach that can be implemented without a huge impact on workload or much teacher training: it is a small step with the potential for a big impact.
- Some of the Zones of Regulation can be ambiguous and need to be more carefully explored, for example the 'Red Zone' is complex because it encompasses a range of different feelings from angry to terrified, and the 'yellow Zone' can mean excited (comfortable) or worried (uncomfortable).
- Zones of Regulation tools and strategies need to be adapted for children with special needs or disabilities: introducing one feeling at a time and enabling children to add their own words to the display helped support such children, as did running smaller intervention groups.
- Children with autism need a lot more dialogue and discussion in order to really understand and use the Zones.
- Children with communication needs not only need to work out what Zone they are in but also whether what they are feeling is a comfortable or uncomfortable emotion, and this may require extra support.

● Conducting a research project can be challenging: day-to-day teaching is never the same, so building in adaptability to the intervention you implement is crucial; for example, allowing teachers to teach sessions at different times of the day and with different intensities did not compromise on the integrity of the approach but improved teacher buy-in.

10 Colour monsters and feelings wheels at Carpenters' Primary

Stephen Goggin and Melissa Hobbs

The children

Our project focused on a group of children in Year 2 who struggled to self-regulate, sometimes exhibiting challenging behaviours, both in the classroom in terms of engagement with learning and interacting with their peers, and in particular at lunchtimes, when they were using a lot of adult time.

We looked at progress and attainment data for these children and found that they tended to be working consistently below expectation. Teachers reported that they were over-dependent on adult input and unwilling to attempt challenges without substantial scaffolding, even struggling to identify the starting point for beginning to solve a problem, or in many cases, to access a basic task (e.g. writing a sentence about a given topic). The same difficulties with solving problems were also seen by the leadership team and midday staff at lunch time, where children would meet with challenges while playing outside, or between themselves, such as friendship problems, and be unable to negotiate these without an adult taking the lead.

We tried to use the Happiness Line to try and engage the children in conversations about their current satisfaction in life (Figure 10.1). This was unsuccessful across the board, as the children in this age group were unable to articulate their feelings and, instead, would mirror the adults' responses and seemed to select an answer that they felt would please the adult. For example, Child TE, when discussing things that make her feel sad, or that she would like to improve at school, said 'I'm happy all the time, I never feel sad.' The adult interviewing her reminded her of a recent time when she had seemed very sad and explained how she knew she had been sad (facial expression, the context of the occasion in which a child had been unkind), to which Child TE said: 'I don't mind, I won't be sad anymore. I want you to be happy with me.' Many of the children interviewed showed concern for the adults' happiness and would reply in a way that they believed would make the adult happy. This was also witnessed during observations in class and in the playground, where children would be inauthentic about their feelings when responding to peers, resulting in difficulties later.

DOI: 10.4324/9781003396796-10

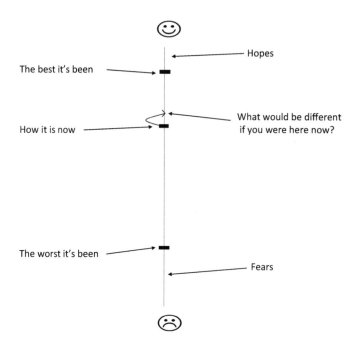

Figure 10.1   Happiness Line

More successful were the observations and profiling software used by the team to assess the needs of the group. The school already buys into an existing commercial SEMH provision, and so had access to a set of online profiling software which had been in use for a number of years. Staff also had a good understanding of what to look for in their classrooms as a result of this. The research team identified key children based on their observations of both classes across the school day, as well as analysis of other data held by the school (attainment, behaviour). These were cross-referenced with the profiles completed by class teachers, and it was found that the same children identified by the research team emerged from the profile data as being well below developmental expectations. The profiles revealed that the key areas that children needed support with were: being able to think while feeling before acting or behaving, knowing they need help before problem-solving and understanding their limitations.

A number of the children in this group had also been the subject of discussions between teachers and parents, either because parents had identified concerns about academic progress or behaviour, or because staff had had concerns of a safeguarding nature. Some examples of these included general presentation and hygiene, access to inappropriate gaming or media or emotional neglect.

In short, these children had a complex set of needs, which staff believed were rooted in SEMH concerns but affected learning and wellbeing across the board.

What we learned from research

Jean Gross (2022) proposed that there are 'four main but overlapping reasons for behaviour problems.' These can be represented by a Venn diagram that groups children according to their ability to manage their own behaviour (see Chapter 1): children who 'can but don't choose to'; children who 'can but temporarily lose it when life gets too much'; children who 'can't and don't know how to' and children who 'can't because of attachment issues/ trauma.' Of course, the way we respond as professionals and caregivers to a child's behaviour in school must be responsive to the underlying cause of their behaviour.

The Year 2 class teachers felt that there was a small group of children possessing the underlying social and emotional skills they need, but would struggle to maintain them at difficult times. For example, Child AH, who was very articulate and could express himself well when calm, but when distressed or under pressure would shut down and find other ways to communicate that he was not okay; example include climbing under tables and banging, but being unable to answer when spoken to, which can often be interpreted by adults as refusal to engage. However, once he had co-regulated with an adult, he would be able to talk in detail about how he was feeling and what he believed had led him to feel and behave in such a way. For us, these patterns of behaviour aligned with the work of Siegel and Bryson (2011), who describe this process as the child's 'thinking brain' being unavailable.

We knew that it would be important to empower the children with the skills and knowledge they need, as well as to create strong connections with key adults in school. Research by Adele Bates (Bates, 2022) showed that children with SEMH needs require constant reassurance that they are valued and worthy and so require this input from adults in a way that is more sustained and consistent than might be required by children who have benefited from secure attachments during their early development.

So it was felt that, as part of children's daily routine, more opportunities to learn the skill of self-regulation would need to be included. These strategies would need to be taught in class, and then supported by adults outside of the classroom (for example at playtimes) as this was when much of the dysregulation – and resulting behaviours – were occurring.

What we did

Class teachers implemented/introduced daily feelings check-ins through class 'Colour Monsters' sessions, based on the book by Anna Llenas (Figure 10.2). This daily activity encouraged children to come in each day, or after a transition, and select the colour monster that most matched their feelings. This allowed classroom adults to explore the reasons for what they were feeling, supporting understanding, self-awareness and articulation.

Teachers also used resources such as a 'feelings wheel' to extend the children's emotion vocabulary. We understood that if the children lacked the skills to express their feelings successfully, they would find other, less useful ways to show what they were thinking and feeling.

In class, teachers ensured that work around emotional literacy was at the heart of all they did, weaving these conversations into the curriculum, but also ensuring this was taught directly through PSHE and RSHE lessons, at least weekly.

Figure 10.2   Colour Monsters display

Additionally, teachers were asked to work through scenarios with the children each day, and encourage problem-solving together (Figures 10.3 and 10.4). For example, after playtime, the teachers would spend time looking at some of the problems that had arisen and facilitate some whole-class problem-solving. The idea behind this was to make sure it was an activity that everyone did together, rather than focusing on a particular individual and increasing the potential for them to experience shame and rejection. This was sometimes an end of the day activity, as the teacher felt something had arisen during class time that would merit a discussion of this kind.

The same strategies and learning were introduced to sports lessons (twice a week) with the sports coach, who tried, as far as possible, to mirror the efforts being made in class, at lunchtime and during interventions. The PE curriculum was also adapted for part of the spring and summer terms, to ensure that there were more opportunities for group problem-solving. The PE teacher entered into these lessons with positivity and gusto and the children responded accordingly.

The most important change that we made for these pupils was ensuring that all staff who worked alongside them, throughout the school day, used therapeutic responses to behaviour that was challenging or inappropriate, rather than sanctions. The strategies used in class, around emotional literacy and problem-solving, were replicated outside of class, so that children were able to apply their learning experiences to real-life situations, for example,

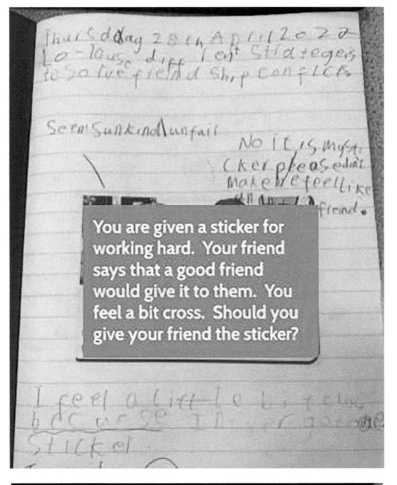

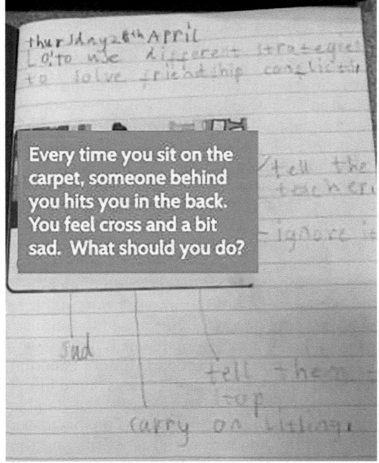

Figures 10.3 and 10.4   Examples of emotional literacy work

disagreements with friends at lunchtime, or difficult conversations about their behaviour with the leadership team. This became more successful and consistent as the year progressed, particularly as teachers practised this skill over time.

With a number of the children, but in particular Child TE, we introduced regular 'special lunches', in which the children could eat with, or spend time with, the same adult. The idea behind this was to discover whether these predictable opportunities to have special time with a consistent adult would have an impact on some of the clingy behaviours that children were displaying, for example, seeking adults at inappropriate times, giving hugs and refusing to let go or pretending to be hurt to get attention.

Another change was implemented at lunchtime: the leadership team, who respond to challenging behaviour, used a 'facilitated problem-solving' approach to support children in reflecting on their behaviour and planning ways to improve interactions next time. This included conversations about feelings and how these link to behaviour.

The impact

A key observation has been that children have developed healthier support-seeking behaviours, both in class, when they become stuck with a piece of work, and in the playground, when there is a dispute between them or another problem that feels too big for them to resolve themselves. The children are also much less needy of adult support and will at least attempt a task before asking for help. Observations revealed that all children had improved their ability to concentrate and work independently, some for sustained periods of time (Figure 10.5). All children were able to make a start on their work, which was a key concern at the outset of the project. All of the children were able to explain the task and could give ideas about what they would write or do next.

We also noticed a significant improvement in terms of the ability to remain focused on the teacher, being able to repeat what the task was and, in most cases, writing or completing the task at hand. For example, during an observation at the beginning of the project Child TE was seen to be: 'Often chatting, not able to focus for long. When asked what she should be doing (the task) couldn't explain …'

An observation of the same child in the second half of the year reported: 'was writing independently, able to say one or two things that they'd seen… then returned to task - improvement in focus and work rate.' While this may not have led to an enormous growth in work outputs, it can certainly be viewed as a step in the right direction and cause for optimism for the future.

Another child with marked improvement was Child AS, who was only able to maintain concentration for a few seconds before becoming distracted or lost, which quickly led to him distracting those around him. He did virtually no written work, and what he did produce was almost illegible to himself and to adults. When an adult scribed for him, he was unable to express any ideas, looking to the adult to provide him with the words and thoughts needed. During the last set of observations Child AS was able to maintain his focus on

Figure 10.5   Children working independently for a sustained time

the teacher, to express one or two ideas to his partner when asked to discuss and then began his writing unprompted. Again, while this amounted to three short sentences, it is clear that progress is beginning.

In fact, Child AS was only able to name two emotions when initially seen (anger and happiness) and was only able to blame other children when getting into disputes, which were a frequent, virtually daily occurrence. Since we introduced the interventions to help him enrich his emotional language, he is rarely seen by senior leaders at break or lunchtime. More important, perhaps, is the way he presents in class: no longer lost and frustrated and more able to join in and communicate.

Teachers mentioned other notable examples of success, including children taking steps to calm themselves down independently, or asking to speak to one of the leadership team, before being sent to them for a challenging behaviour incident. Other children began to initiate conversations about their feelings with a key adult or supporting peers in their behaviour management: 'stop arguing and work together, or we won't get to the finish line – we can do it!' In a recent lesson observation, it was noted that 'Resilience improved – children make mistakes but keep trying to move the hoops. No shouting at each other, just encouragement. Impressive.'

The impact on learning outcomes so far has been limited. We believe this is because the level of social and emotional need was so high that the impact on learning outcomes will be a longer-term goal, as we continue the project into this cohort's Year 3. However, there have been some notable changes which indicate that the work undertaken as part of the project so far is beginning to have a positive impact, and has certainly created an environment for real potential.

Anecdotally, parents have talked about how they have noticed an improvement in their children's moods and views towards school. They have also been pleased that they are contacted less by senior leaders for behaviour issues that have arisen at break and lunchtime.

The leadership team's 'facilitated problem-solving' approach to support children in reflecting on their behaviour and planning ways to improve proved to have a real impact on outcomes. Children displayed greater empathy, and were more willing to share their feelings honestly – even negative ones: for example: 'She [Child TE] got to have lunch with you, and she made me angry when she came into the playground.' As a result of their increased self-awareness, children began to seek help for those times when they experienced difficult feelings. While this may still take up a lot of adult time, it is in fact an important development as it shows children independently identifying emotional issues they face and asking for help.

Wider school impact and next steps

We were able to influence a larger range of teachers than was first expected. We started with other Year 2 teachers and those in Year 6, then got Year 5 involved as well. The main reason that we managed to achieve this was that we offered ideas that were simple, easy to complete and timetabled. No one felt they were being imposed upon and they could see how it fitted in to the school day. In addition to this, all staff were well aware of the emotional needs of the children after the enormous impact of the pandemic. They were happy that we were trying to address the needs that had arisen from this situation rather than simply carrying on or papering over the cracks.

The strategies around emotional literacy and problem-solving both in the classroom and the playground became more successful and consistent as the year progressed. However, this continues to be a work in progress, as there is still a tendency to fall back on familiar, well-established practices in stressful situations. For example, teachers and support staff admitted that they would sometimes move a child's name down on traffic lights or put a child's name under a smiley face when they felt under pressure, as this was seen to stop the behaviour.

We recognised that the school's wider behaviour policy, which still advocates the use of traffic lights, may need to change long term. For children who are within the Jean Gross' descriptor of 'can't and don't know how to', this method of managing behaviour is ineffective, as they lack the ability to do better – no matter how much it is enforced that they have made a bad choice. The severity of the sanction will have little impact. This realisation has ignited a conversation about the school's behaviour policy, and should indeed ignite conversations in all schools about how using sanctions and rewards as external motivators for behaviour is inappropriate for children with SEMH needs. Moving forward, the team is committed to advocating a change in policy and teachers remain committed to adapting their practice.

Reflections

I have found the experience very worthwhile and rewarding. As a class teacher it is all too easy to get wrapped up in the curriculum and the pressure that entails without taking time to consider the needs of each child in the class; whether they are being met on a deep enough level and how this may be resulting in a variety of behaviours in school and indeed at home. The time we have taken to not only think about this ourselves but also to include other members of staff and consider small changes that we can make and different perspectives we can view them from, has already begun to pay dividends. It is gratifying to be here at the start of what I am sure will be a long-term process, not just for the benefits of teaching in a classroom, but hopefully for the future of the children as they make their way in the world and grow into happy, and resilient people, making a positive contribution to society at large.

(**Teacher**)

I have learnt that staff are willing to make choices in the best interest of the children when they are supported to do this in a manageable way. New initiatives, changes to timetable – and the additional planning that this entails – can sometimes be a barrier to staff, who in schools are often already stretched. When our team could see research in action, having an observable impact on the children they teach and work with each day, this was immediately motivating. …. I found the learning around the need to target staff who are not supportive of the vision as much as those who are on board, incredibly useful. This was one of the areas where I have seen the most development in my own leadership, as I have been able to engage colleagues who I would have tended to avoid when co-opting people to support the project.

(**Leader**)

Key takeaways

- When children lie about a negative behaviour it is often because they feel shame or because they don't feel the adult cares about their everyday experiences, rather than because they are trying to 'get away' with something.
- Attention-seeking children are seeking a connection but often lack the skills to make a positive connection: if we view children as connection-seeking, rather than attention-seeking, we immediately put the need before the behaviour.
- Emotional literacy is like any subject: if we don't explicitly model and teach it, most children won't pick it up through osmosis.

- Social and emotional learning should be a thread through all that we do in schools, rather than being restricted to specific lessons on the timetable (though these do have their place as well).
- Reviewing behaviour policies is an absolute priority when considering the needs of SEMH learners: public sanctions fuel guilt and will often propel children into coping behaviours, or make them feel shameful. Instead, they require therapeutic approaches to build relationships that nurture and teach them the skills they need to make better choices in the long term.

11 Older children coaching younger buddies at School 21

Lauren James and Lisa Placks

The children

School 21 is a 4–18 free school in the London Borough of Newham. The school was founded in 2012 and since being established, the community the school serves has become more disadvantaged. Currently, almost 40% of its children are eligible for the Pupil Premium.

During COVID-19 we found a divide was created between different year groups which led to less of a sense of a whole school community. We therefore sought to create a project which helped to foster a sense of community across year groups.

Our target pupils for this project were a Reception class and a Year 4 class. Chowdry and McBride (2017) identified that pupils who display emotional and behavioural difficulties when aged five, if unchallenged, then exhibit further behavioural problems when aged ten. We felt that identifying such behaviours early, working closely with Reception age pupils, we could have a far greater impact on future positive behaviour (Figure 11.1).

At baseline, the Reception pupils displayed a general lack of social and emotional resilience at school (Figure 11.2). All members of staff within Reception observed that pupils were struggling to share and play at age-related expectations with their peers. During whole-class direct teaching sessions children struggled to focus on what was being taught and found it challenging to engage with their partners and to take turns when speaking. Pupils who displayed these behaviours were not able to retain learning. Not all pupils with low social and emotional development showed the same types of behaviour; all, however, showed distress. Some pupils struggled to self-regulate and this behaviour was making it difficult for them to develop relationships with their peers. Those who were not able to self-regulate also had a negative impact on other members of the class.

Within the Year 4 class (Figure 11.3), many pupils displayed behaviours that did not meet age-expected levels for social and emotional skills like resilience. Staff and parents had identified that many pupils were finding school and home life challenging. A high level of additional pastoral support was provided for six children who required additional help before they could be

DOI: 10.4324/9781003396796-11

Figure 11.1   Children working with older peers

How many children in your class find self regulation challenging during a usual school day?

5 responses

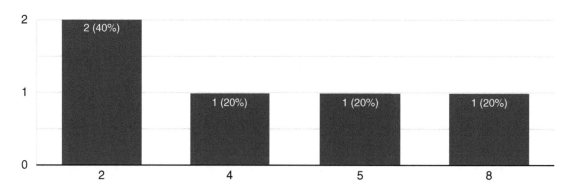

Figure 11.2   Baseline data on self-regulation

ready to learn. It was felt that social and emotional needs were greater than for previous Year 4 classes.

We used the 'Delighted-Terrible' scale (Figure 11.4) to collect initial data about pupils' happiness at school but found that the children's feedback did not always match teachers' observations. Some pupils would report feeling happy although they were clearly showing signs of sadness. We felt this might suggest a lack of emotional literacy.

Figure 11.3   Children sharing a book

'Delighted-Terrible Scale'– Faces

Put a circle around the face that comes closest to showing
how you feel about school.

Figure 11.4   The 'Delighted-Terrible' scale

What we learned from research

The COVID-19 pandemic has had a huge impact on all pupils and has been one of the most stress-evoking periods for families. For many children, COVID-19 was not only a stressful period due to social isolation but also it increased the likelihood that they would experience Adverse Childhood Experiences (ACEs), for example job loss, school closures or family bereavement. Experts see social and emotional learning programs as critical for addressing emotional and mental challenges like these.

In order to design an intervention, we drew heavily on the work of Desautels (2019) whose work on the neuroscience of attachment emphasised the importance of relationships and co-regulation. Co-regulation is firstly modelled by the teacher to the pupil, and this supports the pupil to feel safe and connected within the school. Desautels also highlighted the importance of focusing on pupils' feelings and actively modelling self-regulation techniques. She suggested creating a 'friend-in-need' system to support pupils' regulation and to give them another safe person to talk to, beyond their class teacher.

The EEF (Education Endowment Foundation) report on social and emotional learning (van Poortvliet, Clarke and Gross, 2019) highlighted the importance of explicitly teaching social and emotional literacy. We felt Kuypers' (2021) Zones of Regulation tool could support this approach. We wanted to empower pupils to be able to articulate and communicate their feelings, including enabling pupils who might initially only be able to participate non-verbally.

We also wanted to try out the 'Delighted-Terrible' scale, which was developed and tested by Frank Andrews and Stephen Withey during the 1970s. We felt this tool could support the initial sharing of feelings and enable communication about feelings between the two different age groups we were focusing on.

The EFF report also highlighted the importance of engaging families and community. Parents and carers in both classes were informed about the project and its development by email and newsletter. Surveys were also sent out enabling parents to inform us of any changes at home or if they required additional support.

What we did

Our goal was to encourage pupils to share their emotions by creating a buddy system between Reception and Year 4, with the goal of supporting the development of self-efficacy. The Year 4s would act as coaches for the Reception children, reflecting their role as older pupils and encouraging them to act as leaders.

A series of lessons were planned for both classes that explored the understanding of emotions, including sadness, happiness, excitement and anger. Stories and videos were used as a hook to encourage deep and challenging conversations. Pupils were explicitly taught a range of strategies that they could use when needing to self-regulate during direct teaching sessions. Teachers designed opportunities for pupils to use the vocabulary they were learning in relation to emotions both inside the classroom, in the wider school community and at home.

Within both classes, the teachers ensured that daily check-ins using the Zones of Regulation were embedded at the beginning of each day and after transitions, specifically lunch and break times. If issues were raised by pupils, they were encouraged to consider how to help each other get back to the Green Zone. Pupils who were identified as not meeting age-related expectations were given additional check-ins with pastoral staff; some Reception pupils needed this several times throughout the day.

Figure 11.5   Buddies share a book

Pupils within each class were then buddied up with another child whom they met with at least once a week for an explicit teaching session on emotional literacy and regulation (Figures 11.5 and 11.6). For the Year 4 pupils, this empowered them, putting them in the role of 'coach', whilst for the Reception pupil this was a great way for them to begin to feel they were a part of the school community and to build their confidence around the school. The buddying system was carefully discussed with both class teachers, and those pupils who were identified as below age-related expectations for social and emotional development were paired with a pupil who was at or above age-related expectations in this area.

To ensure the paired session was personalised and not in a huge group, the pairs were split between the two classes and each class was taught a clearly planned lesson. Throughout the lessons pupils sat with their buddies and were asked to take part in partner talk activities. Pupils finished each session by doing an activity with their partner to develop their bond and consolidate learning within the lesson. A medium-term plan was developed for the sessions to ensure progression in the development of skills and strategies. Year 4 have a different lunchtime to the Reception pupils and during their free time the older children were also regularly invited to visit the Reception pupil in their classroom.

At first we thought that the Reception and Year 4 pupils would need to be encouraged, heavily supported and scaffolded to lead successful conversations, but as the pupils are well-rehearsed in talk protocols and practices, this

Figure 11.6   Buddies discuss their emotions

was not the case. Talk flowed and surprisingly Reception held their own and many pupils even asked their older peers complex questions.

One challenge we faced was fitting the sessions into the timetable every week and unfortunately due to other school commitments and staff absences, pupils were not always able to meet as planned on a weekly basis. Sessions were timetabled for 15 minutes, but the reality of swapping classes and having time for the pupil to consolidate their learning with their buddy meant that the session should really have been longer and more like half an hour to 45 minutes.

The impact

By the end of this research project many pupils were able to identify and use strategies to help regulate their emotions independently. These changes were observed by both class teachers, the pastoral team and some of the wider school staff. Key pupils from Year 4 found sessions a beneficial way to support their emotional wellbeing whilst at the same time enabling them to support younger peers. Most Year 4 pupils felt that they had developed meaningful relationships with their younger partner. The majority of the pupils also reported a better knowledge of emotional regulation and could name and explain a range of different strategies that could be used to support them in getting back into the Green Zone when needed.

Teachers noted the impact of the project:

> I have seen many changes in self-regulation within the class. I have noticed that some pupils are now more likely to express their feelings and emotions. Not only this, but the pupils now have different strategies to manage their behaviour and emotions in order to settle down and get back into the Green Zone (e.g. counting to 5, slow breathing and talking to others).

(Year 4 teacher)

Teachers reported that Reception pupils looked forward to seeing their Year 4 buddies, were developing good relationships during the session and shared their skills with their peers. However, some comments made by pupils at the close of the study were concerning, for example: 'I have learned to be happy all the time', 'I have to always be happy' and 'I have learned that you have to be funnier and happy and to be more patient.' The intention was not to say we can't feel or display a range of emotions but to know how to channel these in a safe and developmental way.

The pupils in Year 4 were asked at the end of the project their thoughts regarding whether they felt it had been a successful experience and their responses were generally very positive:

'I've learned that I'm actually capable of controlling my emotions. I learned that Reception people can be more stronger and braver than I thought they would be.'

'I have learned that if you are mad you can breathe in and out four times then you might not be mad but if that did not work then you can breathe ten times and stop what you are doing then 100% sure it will work.'

'What I have learned is that you can calm yourself. I have learned to be honest.'

'I have learned that you can go from red to green and blue to green in so many different ways. I have learned that it's possible to go from blue straight to green.'

'I have learned about myself that I am very kind to little kids and adults.'

Not all the Year 4 pupils were keen on working with younger pupils, however. One said this was because the Reception children got distracted and wouldn't discuss the task. Some, nevertheless, learned from this experience: 'I have learned that [Reception children] are sometimes annoying and sometimes completely change the subject on what we are doing. I learned I can be helpful a bit and lose my patience easily.'

Within the Reception class, Leuven scores for involvement improved greatly over the course of the project, with those scoring less than 3 for involvement going from 11 to 5 pupils. Teachers believe this may be due to the fact that pupils have developed better self-regulation and are therefore able to demonstrate improved concentration in lessons. The wellbeing of pupils in Reception also improved with the number of children scoring less than 3 for wellbeing dropping from 15 to 6. This again could be due to pupils developing better self-regulation so they were able to regulate themselves more easily and express their emotions without becoming distressed. This could be a result of the explicit teaching of the Zones of Regulation and emotions – though it must also be recognised, that pupils developmentally become more able to self-regulate during the Reception year. This is reflected in the early learning goal for personal, social and emotional development, which states that pupils should be able to talk about their feelings and notice feelings in others, to regulate their behaviour and to show kindness with others.

A similar pattern could be seen in the Year 4 class with those scoring less than 3 for involvement going from 13 to 4. Teachers felt this could be linked to self-regulation of the pupils and the fact that the children were more able to recognise their emotions. This improvement was also seen in the pupils' wellbeing with those scoring below 3 decreasing from 21 to 6 pupils.

After the success of the buddying system in this project, additional, much older buddies from Year 9 were identified for two pupils within the Reception class who particularly struggled with their emotional regulation. These relationships are in the early stages, but are very promising, with the younger pupils identifying with their older friends. In addition, the Year 9 pupils are becoming true role models, displaying exemplary behaviour – behaviours which are not always shown when they are amongst their own age group.

Informal visits by Year 4 pupils to Reception pupils during playtimes also seemed to have an impact. Teachers observed pupils interacting with each other in a less formal way and therefore building relationships to support the project. As these buddy friendships blossomed, those Year 4 pupils who did not choose to spend more time with their buddy did not deepen relationships as much.

Unfortunately we only received a small number of responses to parent surveys about the impact of the project (10 out of 52 possible responses). However, some responses relating to their child's behaviour at home led to us being able to work directly with pupils and support the wider family, providing relevant advice and strategies. All parents who responded said that they felt this project had had a positive impact on their child. All parents reported that their child spoke about the project with them. Parents felt that it would be beneficial to repeat this project in following years.

Wider school impact and next steps

We shared the sequence of our project, our expectations and our goals with the wider senior leadership team as we believe this intervention can easily be replicated with other year groups. We made the case for implementation across the school, considering the following aspects which could improve the provision:

1. Consider how to pair the children for future success: should more of a focus be placed on gender, ethnicity, the children's working levels etc. before deciding on the pairings in order to make the project more enjoyable?

2. Use a range of talk protocols, not mainly focusing on partner work – some children in Reception found it overwhelming when talking in pairs so groups might make it more inclusive and comforting.
3. Plan for extra-curricular activities to support engagement: if we could support the children to work together in different ways outside of school hours, would that help to encourage positive relationships in different year groups?
4. Including more emotions, for example, tender (warm-hearted, sympathetic, loving, kind): differentiate and vary vocabulary for different year groups so that they have a wider vocabulary to use for explaining their emotions.
5. Focus on the root causes of negative behaviours: consider what impact some pupils receiving more pastoral support than others might have on outcomes.
6. Ensure that all emotions are seen as normal, so that the pupils do not think they are expected to be happy at all times: many staff and children talk about 'being on green' to feel good, but we all need to understand that we need to have different emotions for different experiences, we just need to know how to talk about them and know how to regulate ourselves.

Reflections

As the class teacher, I have been able to dedicate time each week to support pupils' self-regulation and emotional literacy, and this has empowered me to really put the pupils' wellbeing first which has had a huge impact on my class and their performance during lessons. Working collaboratively with older year groups has had a positive impact on the pupils' sense of belonging in school.

(**Teacher**)

Initially the project felt quite daunting, I hadn't completed high level research for some time. Anxiety crept in, could I do it, would I remember how to do it? The area of study interested me so this was a huge help in staying focused and engaged throughout. I am really encouraged to push this project throughout the school but definitely will need support from others to plan and execute it on a larger scale.

(**Leader**)

Key takeaways

- Consider the idea of pairing classes and pupils to develop peer buddying systems, to support the development of emotional literacy and self-regulation.

- Develop an emotional literacy and emotional regulation curriculum to be delivered alongside peer experiences to support pupils' social and emotional development.
- For those pupils who are working below age-related expectations, provide extra check-in sessions with trusted adults who are able to provide consistency, especially during transitions to new year groups.

Postscript

Jean Gross and Sarah Seleznyov

Reflecting on what the teachers have written in this book, three things strike us most.

One is how effective it is when teachers (or any other professionals, for that matter) are not *told* what to do in their classrooms, but instead supported to identify the real problems they face, research potential solutions, try them out and carefully evaluate the results.

The second is how relatively simple, low-cost interventions can make a big difference. The schools involved in this project did not have to hire extra staff. They did not have to bring in big-name 'trainers.' They did not have to buy new equipment or fancy IT systems.

What they did do, however, was commit teaching and learning time to developing whole-class social and emotional skills. They planned and delivered 30 minutes to an hour of such teaching a week, backed up by routines and practices running through everyday teaching for the rest of the week. And as a result, they found that children were better able to learn, and that less time was wasted sorting out behaviour issues and conflicts.

There has to be a lesson here for other schools struggling with 'coverage' of a crowded curriculum who feel they don't have time for such airy-fairy stuff as helping children understand and deal with their emotions.

Finally, what strikes us most as a result of being involved with this project are the skills, energy and commitment of the teachers involved. They read widely, followed leads, thought carefully about how to work with their colleagues, reflected on successes, learned from failures and wrote up their work in 'proper' research style.

Their project made an enormous difference to many children. It is this, more than anything, that we want to celebrate now, in the hope that their work will inspire other hard-pressed teachers to focus on social and emotional learning – and to make their own difference, in their own classrooms, in their own way.

DOI: 10.4324/9781003396796-12

Resource Bank: Contents

This section contains material adapted from resources created for their project by the teachers who contributed to this book. It also contains a wider set of resources to support social and emotional learning. In the resource bank you will find:

Resource One:
Three lessons on understanding and managing feelings

Resource Two:
Understanding how the brain works: an upper KS2 lesson

Resource Three:
Planning examples for 'Monday morning meetings' and 'Friday round-ups'

Resource Four:
Top picture books for teaching about emotions and guidance on using fiction to explore feelings

Resource Five:
A progression in vocabulary for describing emotions

Resource Six:
A list of top emotion check-ins and guidance on making check-ins meaningful

Resource Seven:
Resources for conflict resolution and playground problems

Resource Eight:
Twenty simple exercises to help children stay calm

Resource Nine:
A progression in social and emotional learning
A list of useful websites

Resource One: Three lessons on understanding and managing feelings

These three PowerPoint lessons have been adapted from a series created by Eilidh Kirkpatrick and Annabel Greyling at New City Primary School. Eilidh and Annabel drew on Leah Kuypers Zones of Regulation framework when creating the lessons, and used picture books suggested by Leah and her team in the Zones 'Book Nook.'

The examples here form part of a longer series of 11 lessons on the Zones of Regulation. You can download the slides for all 11 lessons at www.routledge.com/9781032500720.

The lessons are intended to be used on a whiteboard in PSHE lessons. They include teacher input, links to videos and ideas for independent learning activities.

Understanding and managing feelings

Lesson 1: The upstairs and downstairs brain

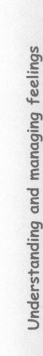

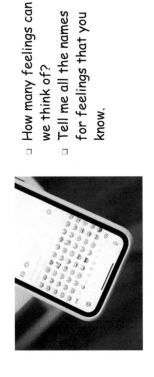

- How many feelings can we think of?
- Tell me all the names for feelings that you know.

It can be helpful to think about our brain as a house. The thinking brain lives upstairs, and the feeling brain lives downstairs.

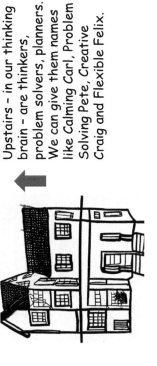

Upstairs – in our thinking brain – are thinkers, problem solvers, planners. We can give them names like Calming Carl, Problem Solving Pete, Creative Craig and Flexible Felix.

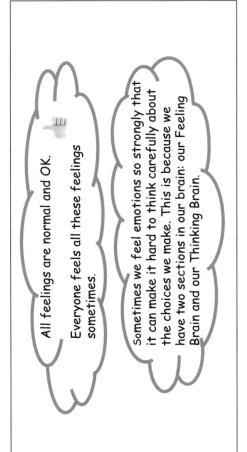

All feelings are normal and OK.

Everyone feels all these feelings sometimes.

Sometimes we feel emotions so strongly that it can make it hard to think carefully about the choices we make. This is because we have two sections in our brain: our Feeling Brain and our Thinking Brain.

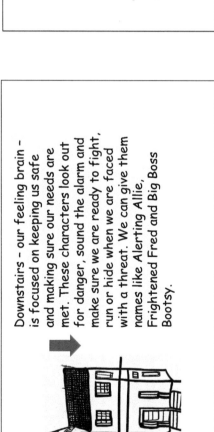

Let's watch a video to find out more about how the thinking brain (upstairs) and feeling brain (downstairs) work together! _The Brain House – BBC Teach._

Downstairs – our feeling brain – is focused on keeping us safe and making sure our needs are met. These characters look out for danger, sound the alarm and make sure we are ready to fight, run or hide when we are faced with a threat. We can give them names like Alerting Allie, Frightened Fred and Big Boss Bootsy.

Flipping your lid

- Sometimes we are in danger and need to react quickly so we can either 'fight' or go into 'flight' mode (run away).
- Like if a huge bear came into your house! In dangerous situations, sometimes our feeling brain protects us.

Flipping your lid

- When you flip your lid, it is like the stairs between your upstairs and your downstairs brain being blocked.
- Your feeling brain takes control and reacts without thinking.
- This isn't always a bad thing.

Flipping your lid

Turn to your partner. Talk about a time when you flipped your lid.

- Sometimes we flip our lids too quickly if we feel a little upset or angry.
- Maybe if we can't find something we're looking for or aren't allowed to do what we want.
- When this happens, we might throw things, be rude or even fight.

Share your ideas

What names did you come up with for your

- Thinking brain characters?
- Feeling brain characters?

Flipping your lid

- Your feeling brain can take control when you feel an emotion strongly.
- This happens to everyone – even teachers!
- But it happens to children more than adults. This is because children's brains don't finish fully growing until they are in their 20s.

Can you draw your own brain house?

<Insert here a newly-drawn image like the first one in this article, or like the children's drawings further down in the article. www.heysigmund.com/how-to-teach-kids-about-the-brain-laying-strong-foundations-for-emotional-intelligence-by-dr-hazel-harrison/ >

Remember your 'thinking' brain characters live upstairs and your 'feeling' brain characters live downstairs.

What will you call them?

<insert image of the brain house created for Lesson 1>

In the last lesson we learned about the upstairs (thinking) brain and the downstairs (feeling) brain.

Can you explain this to your partner?

Can your partner explain to you what it means to 'flip your lid'? When is this a good thing? When is it not such a good thing?

☐ We are going to do this by talking about 'Zones of Regulation'.

☐ There are four Zones of Regulation, and each Zone is connected to different feelings.

Understanding and managing feelings

Lesson 2: An introduction to the Zones of Regulation

☐ We can think most clearly, and make the best choices, when our thinking and our feeling brains are communicating well.

☐ Today we are going to learn about how to help our thinking and feeling brain communicate better when our feelings start to take control. Another word for this is being able to 'self-regulate'.

Green Zone

When we are in the Green Zone we feel calm and happy.

We are curious to explore new knowledge and experiences.

We feel focused on what we are learning or doing.

Yellow Zone

When we are in the yellow Zone we might feel:

- Worried
- Excited
- Frustrated
- Upset
- Silly
- Embarrassed

Zones of Regulation

Green Zone	Yellow Zone
Blue Zone	Red Zone

Blue Zone

When we are in the Blue Zone we might feel:

- Tired
- Sad
- Scared
- Sick

Which Zone might be best for our learning in school?

Green Zone	Yellow Zone
Blue Zone	**Red Zone**

Share your ideas

☐ Group by group, share your ideas with the class.

☐ Can you add anything to your friends' ideas?

Red Zone

When we are in the Red Zone we might feel:

☐ Angry
☐ Overwhelmed
☐ Mad
☐ Out of control

Activity

You are going to work in a group. I will give your group a 'Zone' card : Blue, Green, Yellow or Red

Your group has to come up with ideas. What would this Zone:

Look like? E.g. frowning, head down

Sound like? E.g. yawning, 'I'm tired'

Feel like? E.g. no energy

In the last lesson we learned about the Zones of Regulation

Blue Zone
Green Zone
Yellow Zone
Red Zone

Have you ever got so excited you got into the Red Zone?

Turn to your partner. Talk about a time when you got very excited.

Understanding and managing feelings

Lesson 3: Exploring excitement and anger

- ☐ Which Zone might this child be in?
- ☐ How do you know?
- ☐ Can you name the emotion?

Let's read a story

When Sophie gets angry ... really, really angry

by Mollie Bang

https://youtu.be/dNfd8WF DBAY

- ☐ Which Zones can you spot in the story?
- ☐ How can you tell Sophie is feeling this way?

- ☐ Does Sophie feel the same level of angry throughout the story?
- ☐ Can you think of different ways to label her emotion which also tell us how intensely she is feeling it?

- ☐ Does Sophie look angry all through the story? If not, what does she look like? What Zone is she in?
- ☐ Why do you think Sophie cried?
- ☐ Do we always cry or feel pain when we get angry?
- ☐ Are feeling hurt and being angry the same thing?

Blue Zone Green Zone Yellow Zone **Red Zone**

☐ What Zone is Sophie in at the end of the story?

☐ How did she get herself back to this Zone?

What calm-down strategies might work for us to get us out of the Red Zone and back to the Green Zone?

Let's make a mind-map as a class

Remember it is OK to be in any of the Zones. We have strategies to help us get back to the Green Zone because we learn best there.

Resource Two: Understanding how the brain works: an upper KS2 lesson

This resource consists of

- A lesson plan with a starter, video links, two activities and a plenary
- Resource sheet 1: explaining how the brain works
- Resource sheet 2: roles to cut out
- Resource sheet 3: a job description for the neocortex
- Resource sheet 4: a job description for the limbic system
- Resource sheet 5: a job description for the brain stem and cerebellum (reptilian brain).

Resource sheet 2 provides a script to explain the parts of the brain and their function. Resource sheets 2–5 support a paired or group activity in which children match cut-out roles to the part of the brain they belong to.

The lesson has been adapted from one originally devised by Sarah Davies, a PSHE lead in a Gloucestershire school.

The lesson plan and resource sheets can be photocopied or downloaded from www.routledge.com/9781032500720.

Understanding how the brain works: an upper KS2 lesson

We are learning to: understand why feelings sometimes 'take over' or get out of control.

What I'm looking for is:

- I can describe different parts of the brain and what they do
- I can explain why emotions take us over

STARTER

- Show this short clip from an 'Inside Out' trailer: www.youtube.com/watch?v=WE4ER3cEVrI.
- Ask children to discuss with a partner what it means to lose it.
- Explore with the class whether it is only angry feelings that can make us lose it. Have them think about panic and over-excitement as other examples.

ACTIVITY 1

- Use Resource sheet 1 to explain the parts of the brain and how the feeling brain can sometimes take over.
- Give each pupil a piece of paper (fold into three) and ask them to draw a picture to help them remember each part of the brain, for example:
  neocortex – business-person or army general
  limbic system – a favourite animal showing its feelings
  brain stem/ reptilian brain – any kind of reptile they know

ACTIVITY 2

Ask children what they think 'flipping your lid' means. Establish that it means the same as 'losing it.' Use Part 2 of Resource sheet 1 to demonstrate another way of describing the parts of the brain - the 'hand model.'

Reinforce the learning by showing this film: www.youtube.com/watch?v=2xeDcPBD5Fk.

Have children work in pairs or groups to draw, describe or write down times they have 'flipped their lid', including times when they were overwhelmed by worries or got so excited they couldn't think straight, as well as times when they lost their temper.

PLENARY

Give out cut-out roles and match them to the part of the brain they belong to, to create a 'job description' for the neocortex, limbic system and brain stem (Resource sheets 2–5).

Resource sheet 1

Explaining how the brain works

Part 1

The human brain is made up of three main parts:

- The neocortex, where thinking, imagining and planning take place. We use this part of the brain to think critically, solve problems and make decisions. It is the part of the brain that evolved most recently and is particularly well developed in humans.
- The limbic system, which looks after emotion processing and memory. It includes a part of the brain called the amygdala. The limbic system is said to be the second oldest brain structure. It is sometimes called 'the mammalian brain' because it is present in all mammals.
- The brain stem and cerebellum, which looks after physiological functions that are outside of our conscious control, such as reflexes, breathing, heart rate and digestion. It was the earliest part of the brain to evolve and is sometimes called the 'reptilian brain.'

We can think of these components as the 'upstairs brain' (the neocortex) and the 'downstairs brain'(the limbic system and brain stem). The upstairs brain allows us to think before we act. It helps us make sensible choices and manage our learning.

The 'downstairs brain', in contrast, looks after the basic things that help us survive. It developed at a time when life was dangerous for humans, who had to be ready at all times to react quickly to threats, from wild animals to aggressors from other tribes. So this part of the brain enables us to act fast, without taking time to think and weigh up options. It looks after what is called the 'fight or flight response', when we experience intense feelings and our whole body gets ready to either run away from the threat or fight back.

In the fight or flight response our heart will beat faster, and we breathe faster and more shallowly, so as to get more oxygen. Our stomach may churn, because digestion stops so as to direct all energy and blood flow to the muscles. Our hands and feet may tingle because the blood flow has been redirected to the large muscles. Our throat and chest may feel tight because our body is tensing ready to flee or attack.

When we are in fight or flight mode, our limbic system overrides the neocortex. We go into emotional overdrive. And while this worked well to protect us in caveman times, it often isn't appropriate to the way we live today. Life is much less dangerous, but our evolution hasn't yet caught up with that fact. We are, essentially, still cavepeople – but with the internet.

Nowadays, our feelings can build up and we can end up losing control just as a result of everyday frustrations or worries. This happens to all of us.

Part 2

Another way of describing the brain is the 'hand model', which involves visualising the human brain using one hand. The wrist and palm are the primitive reptilian brain, which controls basic things such as heart rate and respiration. The thumb bent over the palm is the limbic or mammalian brain – the emotional centre. The fingers and knuckles folded over the top represent the part of the brain dedicated to higher-level thinking and decision making: the neocortex or prefrontal cortex. When we are in panic mode the top part of the brain (represented by the fingers) has flipped up. The thinking parts of the brain are no longer in control and the lower parts of the brain that control the fight-flight responses take over. This is 'flipping your lid.'

Resource sheet 2: roles to cut out

Feeling scared and sending fast messages to the brain stem and neocortex to warn of danger and the need to run away
Making decisions after considering all the evidence
Sending messages to the brain stem to tell it to make us breathe faster when there is danger
Controlling our breathing
Feeling angry and sending fast messages to the brain stem and neocortex to say we need to fight
Imagining what might happen in the future
Feeling sad and sending messages to the brain stem to tell it to make our body slow down
Planning how to tackle a problem
Feeling excited and sending messages to the neocortex that it should let us have some fun
Thinking what to say in a conversation
Managing the body systems that digest food
Choosing what to pay attention to
Making our muscles tense up
Sending more blood to our muscles
Sneezing when something gets up our nose

Job description

Neocortex

Your roles will include:

Job description

Limbic system

Your roles will include:

Job description

The brain stem and cerebellum (reptilian brain)

Your roles will include:

Resource Three: Planning examples for Monday morning meetings and Friday round-ups

Pinner Wood Primary, one of the schools involved in the project described in this book, approached teaching about emotions through short weekly Monday morning and Friday afternoon class meetings.

In each Monday morning meeting, a new emotion was introduced and explored. Children came up with strategies for dealing with the feeling.

At the Friday afternoon round-up meeting they reflected on whether they had experienced the feeling during the week, and on their use of self-regulation strategies to manage their feelings.

The planning examples here are about angry feelings.

Monday morning meeting

A planning example from Pinner Wood School
Monday morning meetings are 15 minutes long. Children develop strategies for dealing with different emotions or set goals for the week.

KQ: What strategies can we use when we're feeling angry?	Outcome: Children to talk about strategies they can use when feeling angry.
Starter: Ask the children to sit in a circle on the carpet. Show the children three pictures of children looking angry. Make sure that these are varied, e.g. one person with their face scrunched/ clenching their fists, one stamping their feet and one sitting in a corner. If applicable, ask the children what zone of regulation the people are feeling? Otherwise, ask the children how the people are feeling. Ask the children for synonyms for the word angry, write these down and display them in the classroom. Main teaching: Ask the children to talk to their partner about what advice they would give to someone who is feeling angry. What strategies can they think of? At this point, model a variety of techniques including: - Clenching and releasing fists - Mountain breathing (where you trace between your fingers with your alternative hand, breathing in and out as you move up and down your fingers) - Lifting something heavy - Speaking to a trusted friend or adult - Having a drink of cold water - Taking some time outside Plenary: Ask the children to think independently about a time when they have felt angry. How did they overcome these feelings? What strategies work best for them? Ask the children to feed back to the class if they wish.	

Friday Round Up

A planning example from Pinner Wood School
The Friday Round Up is about 15 minutes long. It is paired with the Monday morning meeting and is a chance for the class to reflect.

KQ: What strategies have you used this week when feeling angry?	Outcome: Children to talk about strategies they have used when feeling angry.

Starter: Ask the children to sit in a circle on the carpet.
Show the children three pictures of children looking angry (make sure that these are the same as those that were shared during the Monday morning meeting earlier that week).

Main teaching: Ask the children to reflect individually on the week that they have had.
Were there any times where you felt angry or frustrated?
What led you to feel that way?
What did you do? What strategies did you use? Which were the most effective and why?

At this point, revisit the strategies that were taught on Monday including:
- Clenching and releasing fists
- Mountain breathing (where you trace between your fingers with your alternative hand, breathing in and out as you move up and down your fingers)
- Lifting something heavy
- Speaking to a trusted friend or adult
- Having a drink of cold water
- Taking some time outside
Ask the children to feed back to the class if they wish. Take this opportunity to share some successes of the week where children have self-regulated well.

Plenary: Moving forward, ask the children to think about the next week and what they can continue to do to develop their self-regulation.

Resource Four: Top picture books for teaching about emotions and guidance on using fiction to explore feelings

These resources list favourite books for teaching about emotions, and provide guidance on how to use them.

The booklist includes picture books to help explore the specific emotions of anger, fear and anxiety, happiness and excitement, sadness, disappointment, pride, jealousy and guilt. It also lists useful books about feelings more generally.

The guidance suggests ways of using the books in PSHE and English lessons, and provides prompts to promote class or group discussion.

Top picture books for teaching about emotions

Anger	Fear/anxiety	Happiness, excitement
When Sophie gets angry, by Molly Bang	*Ruby's worry*, by Tom Percival	*When I'm feeling happy*, by Tracey Moroney
Behaviour matters: tiger has a tantrum, by Sue Graves	*Little mouse's big book of fears*, by Emily Gravett	*The happy owls*, by Celestino Piatti
Fergal is fuming!, by Robert Starling	*Franklin goes to the hospital*, by Paulette Bourgeois and Brenda Clark	*Have you filled a bucket today?*, by Carol McCloud
When I'm feeling angry, by Tracey Moroney	*Chester the brave*, by Audrey Penn	*The jar of happiness*, by Alisa Burrows.
Ravi's roar, by Tom Perceval	*When I'm feeling nervous*, by Tracey Moroney	*Augustus and his smile*, by Catherine Rayner
I really want to shout, by Simon Philip	*The huge bag of worries*, by Virginia Ironside	*Happy!*, by Pharrell Williams
Angry Arthur, by Hiawyn Oram and Satoshi Kitamura	*Silly Billy*, by Anthony Browne	*Today I feel silly, and other moods that make my day*, by Jamie Lee Curtis
When I see red, by Britta Teckenstrup	*Big bad bubble*, by Adam Rubin	

Sadness	Disappointment	Pride, jealousy and guilt
Blue, by Sarah Christou	*When I'm feeling disappointed*, by Tracey Moroney	*Cornelius*, by Lio Lionni
When I'm feeling sad, by Tracey Moroney	*The disappointment dragon: learning to cope with disappointment*, by K.I. Al-Ghani	*When cucumber lost his cool*, by Michelle Robinson
The sad book, by Michael Rosen		*Get lost*, by Laura Jennifer Northway
I'm sad, by Michael Ian Black		
A shelter for sadness, by Anne Booth		
Alexander and the terrible, horrible, no good, very bad day, by Judith Viorst		

General
Great big book of feelings, by Mary Hoffman
A book of feelings, by Salvatore Rubbino
The colour monster, by Anna Llenas
My many colored days, by Dr Seuss
Tough guys (have feelings too), by Keith Negley
Today I feel … an alphabet of emotions, by Madalena Moniz
How do you feel?, by Anthony Browne

Guidance on using fiction to explore feelings

These are some suggestions for different ways of using fiction (picture books and other types of texts) to explore feelings.

- Use the book to collect words for emotions that can be shared on a feelings wall.
- Plot characters' feelings on an axis of emotion, where the horizontal axis represents time (from the beginning to the end of the book, for example or over a chapter) and the vertical axis represents intensity of emotion, from low to high.
- Hotseat fictional characters: one child sits in the centre in the 'hotseat' and other children ask them what they were thinking and feeling and how that influenced the choices they made.
- Have children annotate a text with emojis showing characters' emotions at different parts of the story.
- Put up an image of a character and ask children to label what's happenng beneath the surface (thoughts, feelings) and what it looks like on the outside (words, actions).
- Have the children make props for a story, like their own 'worry dolls' after reading Anthony Browne's *Silly Billy* picture book.
- Have them create lolly-stick puppets of characters and re-enact scenes. For example, working in pairs to take on the role of Billy or a Worry Doll and developing a short role-play to be performed in a small puppet theatre.
- Have older children buddy with a younger class. The older children read a picture book about a feeling and create their own book, which they then share with the younger children. For example, they might read *Big bad bubble* and create a book about their childhood fears, sharing this with the buddy class and helping the younger children write their own pages for the book.
- Follow a story with an open question, like 'What does this story make you wonder about?' Children can talk in pairs and come up with topics they would like to discuss as a class. The class then votes to choose one topic from all the ideas, and then have a 15-minute discussion on that topic.

Discussion prompts for talking about a book

- How might they be feeling?
- How can you tell?
- When was a time you felt …?
- Is this a comfortable or uncomfortable feeling?
- What makes you feel better if you feel this way?
- Can you use a word from the story to explain how you felt when….?

Sentence stems to help children structure their responses

- I wonder if that character felt _____ because _____.
- I can tell they felt _____ because _____.
- That character felt _____ and I have felt like that too when _____.

Examples of discussion questions

Feelings in general

Do the words that we say always show the feelings that we have?
How can you be sure that someone feels the way they say they do?
Have you had an instance when what you said doesn't match how you felt?

Anger

Can you be angry without looking angry?
Are feeling hurt and being angry the same thing?
Can feeling angry be useful?

Fear

Have you ever hidden your fear from a friend? Why or why not?
Why do you think someone would hide their fear from another person?
If people think you are not scared, are you still scared?

Pride and jealousy

Should people be proud of skills they have even if they are born with them?
Can feeling jealous ever be useful?
What does it mean when we say 'pride comes before a fall'?

Resource Five: A progression in vocabulary for describing emotions

This resource provides a detailed progression for one aspect of social and emotional learning: the ability to understand and use a wide range of words to describe feelings.

It lists words which might be taught in each year group in school, and includes words for

- Happiness
- Sadness
- Disgust
- Anger
- Fear
- Surprise/anticipation
- Guilt and shame
- Calm/alertness
- Feeling excluded/included
- Feeling motivated/less motivated

The resource can be used to develop a school's PSHE or RSE curriculum so as to create a sequenced and comprehensive approach to teaching children how to understand and describe how they or others are feeling.

A progression in vocabulary for describing emotions

	EYFS	Year 1	Year 2	Year 3	Year 4	Year 5	Year 6
Happiness	happy	cheerful	proud pleased	hopeful thankful	joyful relieved satisfied delighted	optimistic amused overjoyed carefree	content ecstatic jubilant fulfilled elated
Sadness	sad hurt	unhappy upset	disappointed blue	miserable gloomy	dejected downcast glum	pessimistic sorrowful heartbroken grieving disheartened	despairing forlorn depressed despondent dispirited
Disgust				disgusted	revolted	horrified	repelled appalled
Anger	angry cross mad	jealous	annoyed frustrated	furious irritated	sulky	infuriated raging disapproving exasperated	hostile indignant resentful critical irate
Fear	scared worried	frightened afraid	anxious fearful	terrified panicky	suspicious tense jittery	nervous overwhelmed helpless	apprehensive stressed threatened agitated
Surprise/ anticipation	excited	surprised	amazed	startled	shocked	astonished	dismayed perplexed bewildered
Guilt and shame			ashamed	guilty	embarrassed	regretful	remorseful
Calm/ alertness	excited sleepy	peaceful relaxed	bored tired	energetic	soothed	withdrawn wary	serene tranquil pensive focused vigilant
Feeling excluded/ included	lonely	welcomed		accepted respected	isolated	rejected humiliated valued	ridiculed persecuted alienated
Feeling motivated/less motivated	interested	frustrated	confident confused	motivated distracted	curious determined	eager persistent apathetic	hesitant engaged resilient passionate inspired indifferent

Resource Six: A list of top emotion check-ins and guidance on making check-ins meaningful

These resources describe a range of different ways in which children can be asked to reflect on how they are feeling, at points within the school week or day.

The list of top emotion check-ins expands on the Zones of Regulation check-ins used by many of the teachers contributing to this book, providing additional ideas that are curriculum-linked or highly visual.

The accompanying guidance suggests that varying the type of check-in used helps maintain children's interest and engagement. It provides ideas on following up check-ins with opportunities for children to explore the reasons for their mood and to receive support where needed.

A list of top emotion check-ins

Feeling faces (early years)	Have children make 'feeling faces' from paper plates. They choose one to hold up, to show how they are feeling.
Feelings stones (early years)	Paint different feeling faces on stones for children to choose from.
Mood meter (early years)	Have a big display of four coloured squares: (happy, angry, sad, calm) to which children attach their own laminated photo.
Spoon puppets (early years)	Make your own Colour Monster wooden spoon puppets, for children to hold up.
Emojis	Have children use https://emojifinder.com/ or make their own emojis to show how they are feeling.
Memes	Make a display of memes from the internet (for example, cats who look as if they are showing different emotions) and have children choose the meme that best represents their mood.
Thumbs up	Ask children to put their thumbs up if they are feeling good, down if not so good, or sideways if in between.
Weather	Ask the children what their mood might be if it was the weather. For example, if angry it could be a thunderstorm.
Lolly sticks	Children put a lolly stick with their name on into a pot. The pots can be labelled with characters from Pixar's 'Inside Out', for example.
Song/movie check-in	Ask the children: If your current mood were a song or movie, what would it be? For example, if they are feeling good then their song could be 'Happy' by Pharrell, or if they are grumpy their movie could be 'The Grinch.'
Curriculum-related check-ins	Use check-ins linked to a topic of study, e.g. 'choose a landform to represent your mood today' (river, volcano, jagged rocks etc.), 'what sport resembles your mood right now?' (marathon, sprint etc.).
Journalling	Have children write a daily journal, which is confidential and not looked at by adults unless the child chooses to share. It can be useful for children to journal on Mondays to reflect on their weekend, identify their current mood and look ahead to the next few days. They can then be taught a wellbeing strategy to use, and on Friday reflect in their journal on how useful they found it and whether they want to add it to their own wellbeing toolbox.
Zones of Regulation check-ins	After teaching children about the four Zones of Regulation and their associated emotions, create a display of the Blue, Green, Yellow and Red Zones to which children can attach a peg with their name written on it.

Zones of Regulation sensory check-ins for children with SEND	Have children use bottles filled with food colouring to spray a colour indicating their mood onto paper.
	    Ask them to pick up a sticky toy and 'splat' it onto a particular coloured sheet on the wall.
	    Have them use split-pin spinners with four coloured, labelled quadrants.

Guidance on making check-ins meaningful

Asking children to reflect on or share how they are feeling at the start of the school day or after lunchtimes or breaktimes is a useful way of helping them develop self-awareness, and use a wide range of vocabulary for emotions.

Such check-ins can also be an engaging way for children to start class, a ritual through which they establish a sense of belonging and community, and an assessment tool that helps adults take the temperature of the class and identify children who aren't going to be ready to learn.

But they need to be used in meaningful ways, leading to action where it is needed.

Children should be taught that their emotions signal that something important is at stake. When we feel sad, it means something important is gone. When we feel angry, it means something important was taken away – from us or someone important to us. When we feel afraid, it means something important is being threatened.

When they share their emotions, children need time to try to understand the source of their mood, so ask them to talk briefly with a partner about why they chose the feeling and what it might be signalling.

Pair children as 'listening buddies' for this exercise, keeping to the same pairs for a term so as to build trust in each other.

Try back-to-back as well as face-to-face conversations after check-ins. Children may find it easier to talk about how they are feeling this way.

Notice the children who signal that they are unhappy, anxious or angry first thing in the morning and try to give them some 1–1 time with an adult – maybe giving them some marker pens and big paper to draw a picture of the feeling and what led to it.

You could also try giving the child a double-sided laminated sheet – pink on one side, green on the other – if they have identified as sad or angry after breaktimes or lunchtimes. Ask them to draw on the pink side the problem they are facing. Later (not in learning time), talk with them so they come up with possible solutions. They choose one and draw it on the green side of the sheet.

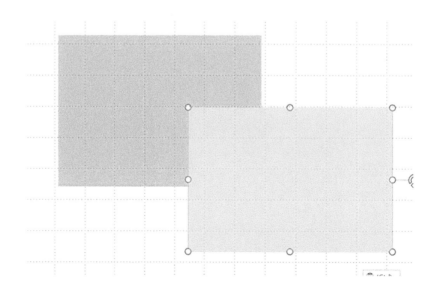

Sometimes ask for multiple emotions in a check-in, instead of just one. We are capable of feeling many different emotions, sometimes simultaneously or in rapid succession. Children might feel angry about something their sibling did, excited about that afternoon's football game, and worried about tomorrow's maths test. They might even feel multiple emotions about the same thing, so we might ask questions like

- Which three emojis tell the story of your day so far?
- Thinking back on the past week, when was a time when you felt each of the following emotions?

Above all, try to vary the type of check-ins you use, once children have had several weeks of practice in using one type. If the format is always the same it can easily become a routine to which they give little thought and attention. It works best if you develop a repertoire of different check-ins from which you – or the class – can choose, from week to week.

Resource Seven: Resources for conflict resolution and playground problems

These resources consist of

- Three PowerPoint lessons to help tackle problems in the playground: one on empathy, one on playing together, and one on dealing with the problems that children experience. The lessons have been adapted from those created by Cubitt Town Primary for the project they describe in this book
- Guidance on developing children's conflict resolution skills, including a playground 'Peace Path'
- A template for a Peace Path developed at Cubitt Town Primary

The lessons and template can all be downloaded at www.routledge.com/ 9781032500720.

The three lessons on playground problems were developed for children in Years 3 and 6. Lesson 3 provides alternative slides for each year group.

SUPPORT MATERIAL

Empathy helps us with this guideline

☐ Show active listening
☐ Use positive body language
☐ Agree and disagree politely
☐ Be willing to change our mind
☐ Build, challenge, clarify and summarise ideas
☐ Bring others into the conversation
☐ Give reasons for your opinions

Empathy

Empathy is the ability to put yourself in another person's shoes. This allows you to understand the feelings of others as if they were yours.

Let's watch a film about empathy.

www.youtube.com/watch?v=ka5pSiyJ5ok

These are our class guidelines for talking and working together

☐ Show active listening
☐ Use positive body language
☐ Agree and disagree politely
☐ Be willing to change our mind
☐ Build, challenge, clarify and summarise ideas
☐ Bring others into the conversation
☐ Give reasons for your opinions

Playground problems Lesson 1

Empathy

Here are some pictures suggesting empathy

Today's takeaway!

Empathy is the ability to put yourself in another person's shoes. This allows you to understand the feelings of others as if they were yours.

Try this out: Practise showing kindness to your friends and family if you think they are feeling sad.

Why might empathy be important?

Let's watch another film clip, from the film 'Wonder.'
www.youtube.com/watch?v=zJMCctR8ivc

How can we feel empathy for the boy in 'Wonder' if we don't have the same experience?

Activity

1. Draw your own picture that shows empathy.

2. When I tell you, share your picture with a partner and explain what it shows.

3. Tell your partner about a time when you think you showed empathy.

Look at these pictures

Talking point

'Playtime is happier when everyone has someone to play with.'

You are going to work in trios (threes)
Two of you will have a discussion about the talking point
The third person will observe then summarise the discussion

Remember to use sentence starters like
- ☐ I agree with the point that x made because ...
- ☐ I disagree because ...
- ☐ Building on what x said, I think ...
- ☐ To sum up, what you thought was ...

Playground problems Lesson 2

Playing together

Let's talk as a class about the pictures

Use these sentence starters

- ☐ I see ...
- ☐ I think ...
- ☐ I wonder ...

Copyright material from Jean Gross and Sarah Seleznyov (Eds) (2024), *Improving Behaviour and Wellbeing in Primary Schools*, Routledge

What ideas do you have about this situation?

You see someone alone at playtime, and they look lonely. How could you encourage them to play?

Let's collect your ideas on the whiteboard.

Today's takeaway!

All of us have had times when we felt lonely or left out. It's an uncomfortable feeling. We can show empathy and invite anyone who is lonely into our games.

Try this out: Notice anyone who might be feeling lonely in the playground and encourage them to play.

Remember our class guidelines for talking and working together

- ☐ Show active listening
- ☐ Use positive body language
- ☐ Agree and disagree politely
- ☐ Be willing to change our mind
- ☐ Build, challenge, clarify and summarise ideas
- ☐ Bring others into the conversation
- ☐ Give reasons for your opinions

Which of these do you think would work for your age group?

- ☐ Ask them how they're feeling
- ☐ Ask if they are okay – check in with them
- ☐ Ask them to play with you
- ☐ Tell some jokes

- ☐ Say 'Do you want to be my friend?'
- ☐ Say 'Why don't you join our game?'
- ☐ Ask 'What do you want to play?'
- ☐ Say 'You're welcome to play with us if you want'

Starter: how many words do you know for angry feelings?

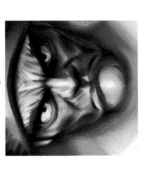

Let's make a list of common problems in the playground that make us angry or upset

Playground problems Lesson 3

Dealing with problems in the playground

Last year, Year 3 made this list. Are ours still the same?

☐ Making rude faces
☐ Losing your friends
☐ Having no one to play with
☐ Bullying
☐ Kids being unkind – pushing
☐ Being left out of a game on purpose

☐ Not being allowed to play a game
☐ Not being allowed to play because they're different
☐ Someone doesn't want to be your friend
☐ Name calling
☐ Other years not being kind
☐ Punching and hitting

What can you put in your toolbox to tackle problems like these? Talk to your partner then let's make a list.

Today's takeaway!

Playground problems seem to stay the same every year. Maybe we can make this year different.

Try this out: Try out some of the ideas in your toolbox to deal with playground problems.

Last year, Year 6 made this list. Are ours still the same?

- ☐ Rumours (spreading, gossiping)
- ☐ Being left out of a game
- ☐ Discriminated against
- ☐ Name-calling
- ☐ Ignoring each other
- ☐ Physical violence
- ☐ Being rude to each other (verbal abuse)
- ☐ Swearing – foul language

Have we got all these ideas in our toolbox?

- ☐ Go and talk to a friend
- ☐ Play a different game that you enjoy
- ☐ Focus on breathing
- ☐ Drink of water
- ☐ Find somewhere quiet/not busy in the playground (breathe/make noise)
- ☐ Go and speak to an adult
- ☐ Find somewhere to lie down – watch clouds – try and spot any shapes
- ☐ Count to 10
- ☐ Stop thinking about it – try and let it go

Guidance on developing children's conflict resolution skills

Begin by exploring the different perspectives involved in conflicts, using films such as

- Seeing both sides of a story: www.bbc.co.uk/programmes/p011n8cj
- Conflict resolution: www.brainpop.com/health/personalhealth/conflict resolution/?utm_source=youtube&utm_medium=organic-social&utm_campaign=free-stuff&utm_content=conflict-resolution

Teach children sentence starters they can use when they find themselves in conflict with each other.
  In the early years these can be simple

- I didn't like it when you ..
- It made me feel …
- I'm sorry that I made you feel …

With older children you can teach a sequence of steps for conflict resolution. This sequence is taken from the Peaceful Problem-Solving process in the SEAL (Social and Emotional Aspects of Learning) resources (www.sealcommunity.org).

What's the problem?	The problem as I see it is …
How do you both feel?	I felt … when … because … I think you might have felt … So you're saying to me that … (Say it back)
Think of some solutions	I would like… We could try … or … or …
If you're stuck	This isn't working … maybe we need a referee to help us sort it out

A poster of these prompts can be displayed in a corner of the classroom set aside for resolving conflicts.
  You can also spray or hand paint a 'Peace Path' onto the playground surface (or in a corner of the school hall), with footprint markings where each child can place their feet.
  Children progress along the Peace Path, standing across from each other on opposite sides and following a sequence painted alongside (What's the problem? How do you both feel? Think of some solutions).
  Alternatively, you can simply designate an area of the playground for conflict resolution and display a large, laminated Peace Path poster nearby.
  It works best if you involve children and parents in designing and making your Peace Path and then take classes out to role play/practise using it.

A template for a Peace Path poster

.... Primary School

Peace Path	What I can do/ say
Step 1 Calm down	*Take a deep breath* *Calm down (count to 10)* *Go somewhere quieter*
Step 2 How do you feel?	*I feel …* *I'm feeling…*
Step 3 Express yourself!	*I would feel better if …* *I hear that you …* *When … I feel …*
Step 4 Make a plan	*How do we make this right?* *Next time …* *Next time I will …* *Next time we can …*
Step 5 Resolution	*Agree …* *From now on …* *Disagree –* **back to Step 2**

Resource Eight: Twenty simple exercises to help children stay calm

This resource provides a range of self-regulation strategies children can use to help them manage their feelings. They include breathing exercises and relaxation techniques.

Several have links to videos demonstrating the technique in action.

Some are more suitable for younger children and some for older children.

A school might want to build teaching the exercises into a sequenced curriculum suitable for different year groups.

Twenty simple exercises to help children stay calm

The film *Just Breathe* gives children an excellent introduction to self-regulation through relaxed breathing: https://youtu.be/RVA2N6tX2cg.

Here are the 20 exercises.

Basic belly breathing	Children place one hand close to but not touching their nose and the other on their belly. Have them breathe in deeply so they can feel their bellies expand. As they exhale, they can feel the warm air hit their hand.
	www.youtube.com/watch?v=RiMb2Bw4Ae8&t=94s
Belly buddies (early years)	Give every child a small stuffed animal toy to be their own 'belly buddy', and have them give it a name. For a few minutes each day have the children lie down on a rug, putting the toy on their tummy and watching it rise and fall as their lungs move, counting to three with every breath.
	https://youtu.be/bW5ly4nUcWl
Bubble breathing	Imagine your favourite colour or a colour which helps you to feel calm. Take a breath in and imagine you are breathing in this colour. As you breathe out, imagine blowing a big bubble made of this colour.
	https://youtu.be/rRuqxR5oXJM

Wiggle breathing 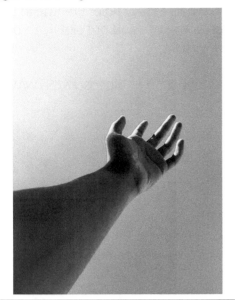	Stand up and, as you take a deep breath in, lift an arm or leg and wiggle it. As you breathe out, take your arm or leg back to its original position.
Hot chocolate breathing 	Pretend to hold your cup of hot chocolate in both hands in front of you. Breathe in deeply the smell of the chocolate. And then blow out to cool it down so you can drink it. Do this to the count of five. https://youtu.be/ylB9Bc1Vt1s
Deep-dive breathing 	Breathe in while counting slowly to four, hold your breath while you count slowly to four, and breathe out for another four counts. Once you've got it, try holding your breath for a few more seconds.

Whale breathing 	Cup your hands around your mouth to make a whale's blow hole. Breathe in slowly through your nose and out slowly through your blow hole. www.gonoodle.com/videos/ywe97w/whale-breath
Bee breathing 	Put your fingers in your ears. Breathe in slowly… breathe out making the sound of a humming bee mmmmmmmm … Repeat five times www.gonoodle.com/videos/72GyKY/bee-breath
Snake breathing 	Take a deep breath in through your nose. Breathe out through your mouth, making a hissing sound. Repeat five times. www.gonoodle.com/videos/lYVWAX/snake-breath
Giraffe breathing 	Picture a giraffe. Trace the giraffe's long neck up … and down, breathing slowly as you go. Repeat five times.

Elephant breathing to re-energise	Stand up with your feet wide apart. Put your hands together to make an elephant's trunk and dangle them between your legs. Breathe in and raise your arms. Breathe out and lower your arms again. Repeat. www.gonoodle.com/videos/a2voVw/ elephant-breath

5-finger breathing/starfish breathing	Stretch your fingers out (in the shape of a starfish) Using the index finger on your other hand, trace each finger in turn UP (breathe in slowly through your nose) then DOWN (breathe out slowly through your mouth). Repeat with the other hand. https://youtu.be/HQVZgpyVQ78

Box breathing	Breathe slowly in and out while watching the ball expand and contract inside a box in this film. www.youtube.com/watch?v=woQPHciR5ec
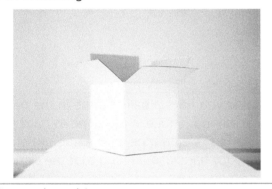	
Square breathing	You will need small squares of paper (post-its work well too). Start with the bottom left corner and trace your finger along the side going up. While doing this take in a deep breath. Then move your finger from the top left corner to the top right corner. This represents holding the breath for four seconds. Bring your finger down (from the top right corner) to the bottom right corner. As you do this, slowly exhale. Finally, bring your finger along the bottom edge of the square to your starting corner. This represents holding in between breaths for four seconds. Repeat 3–5 times. https://youtu.be/jsrf_luItRQ www.youtube.com/watch?v=bF_1ZiFta-E

Hand signals 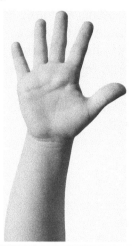	Older children can use hand signals. The hand signals are as follows: palms up to breathe in, palms out to hold the breath, palms down to breathe out slowly. Try doing about five total breaths on a regular basis.
Rapid resets – Pushing against the wall 	Push hard against a wall with both hands.
Slimy hands for muscle relaxation 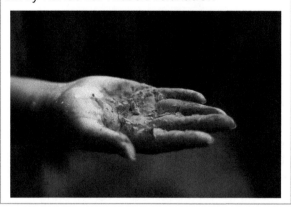	Imagine you have a ball of slime in the palm of each hand. Squeeze the slime as hard as you can as you breathe in. Breathe out and open your hands, imagining that the slime has spread across your hands. Repeat this a few times.

Melt relaxation exercise	Imagine yourself melting after freezing up.
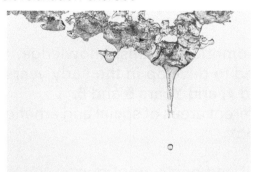	www.gonoodle.com/videos/r2rMeX/melting
Turtle time 	Teach children to hold their hands together above their heads then put their heads down on their desks, making the shape of a turtle in its shell. They can do this whenever they feel angry/panicky/upset, take three deep breaths and think calming thoughts ('I can calm down', 'I am OK', 'I can think of solutions to my problem', 'I am good at solving problems'). When they feel calmer, they can come out of their shell.
Glitter jar/mind jar 	Shake a lidded jar filled with water, a drop of washing-up liquid, a teaspoon of glycerine, and some red glitter. Breathing slowly, watch as the glitter settles to the bottom. www.bbc.co.uk/cbbc/thingstodo/mood-jar

Resource Nine: A progression in social and emotional learning

This resource describes the social and emotional skills, knowledge, and understanding children might be expected to develop in the early years, in primary school Years 1 and 2, Years 3 and 4, and Years 5 and 6.

The skills are grouped under the five different areas of social and emotional learning described in Chapter 1 of this book:

- Self-awareness: understanding oneself and one's emotions
- Self-management: regulating/ managing one's actions and emotions
- Social awareness: understanding those around us and showing empathy
- Relationship skills: interacting with others in a positive and effective way
- Responsible decision-making: making decisions and taking actions as a member of society with rights and responsibilities

The resource can be used to develop a programme of social and emotional learning in school. Leaders might map existing PSHE/ RSE teaching resources and wider learning opportunities against the progression, to create a comprehensive curriculum in which new learning builds on what has gone before.

The progression is based on the learning objectives within the Social and Emotional Aspects of Learning (SEAL) resources that were developed for national use some years ago under a former government (www.sealcommunity.org).

A PROGRESSION in social and emotional learning

Based on the work of Dr Julie Casey and linked to the SEAL curriculum (www.sealcommunity.org)

Self-awareness	Early Years Foundation Stage	Y1+2	Y3+4	Y5+6
Feelings of belonging	Knows and plays with most of the people in the class/group.	Can communicate about people who are important to him/her.	Can talk about why it is important for everyone to belong to a group, and how it feels to belong.	Understands the effects of change and loss on feelings of belonging.
Perception of self-efficacy	Can make choices for him/herself.	Understands that he/she has the power to make choices (e.g. about behaviour and friendships).	Understands that he/she can influence outcome by his/her choices.	Understands that he/she can change things (e.g. in school) by challenging them appropriately.
Knowing and valuing self	Can tell you why he/she is special.	Can identify what he/she is good and not so good at. Can identify his/her strengths as a learner.	Can talk about his/her personality, giving examples (e.g. if he/she likes surprises). Uses his/her learning strengths in the classroom.	Knows and accepts his/her strengths and weaknesses and values self. Knows him/herself as a learner and uses strengths and works on weaknesses.
Recognising, labelling and understanding feelings	Can identify and express basic emotions.	Can identify and express a range of feelings, indicating intensity.	Can identify and predict an increasing range of feelings.	Can identify and express a broad range of feelings, including mixed feelings.

Self-management	Early Years Foundation Stage	Y1+2	Y3+4	Y5+6
Knowledge and understanding that support feeling management	Understands that all feelings are OK, but not all behaviours are OK.	Recognises the internal and external effects of anger, and how it can overwhelm us.	Understands the triggers, and physical effects, of anger and why it is important to calm down before being overwhelmed.	Understands anger triggers, why they can overwhelm and the consequences of uncontrolled anger.
Impulse control	Demonstrates some ability to control impulses, e.g. waiting turn.	Can identify when he/she has acted impulsively, and when he/she has thought his/her actions through.	Can control impulses (stop and think before acting) even when angry or stressed.	Can control impulses in a range of situations and make positive choices.
Skills and strategies for managing uncomfortable feelings/ promoting positive feelings	Uses appropriate strategies to manage emotions (such as relaxing him/herself or doing something different) with support.	Uses appropriate strategies to calm down and manage emotions (such as relaxing him/herself/ doing something different/ thinking differently) with or without support.	Uses appropriate strategies to calm down and manage emotions in an increasing range of situations and with increasing independence.	Uses appropriate strategies to calm down, manage a range of emotions and change uncomfortable feelings independently.
Social awareness	**Foundation Stage**	**Y1+2**	**Y3+4**	**Y5+6**
Knowledge (social cognition)	Understands that all people are equally important and deserving of respect. Understands that everybody has the same range of feelings.	Understands that all people are equally important and deserving of respect. Recognises that there can be more than one way to view, or feel about a situation.	Understands that all people are equally important and deserving of respect. Understands that intolerance of difference can lead to bullying and can identify bullying behaviours.	Understands that all people are equally important and deserving of respect. Can explain people's behaviour with reference to what they might be feeling and thinking.

Understanding feelings and points of view of others	Can tell when other people are angry, happy or sad.	Can tell if other people are feeling a range of basic emotions. Can see a situation from somebody else's point of view.	Can tell if others are feeling a range of emotions. Can see a range of situations from someone else's point of view.	Can recognise a range of feelings in other people, including more subtle ones. Can see a situation in which they are involved from another person's point of view.
Motivation and skills to help others	Demonstrates spontaneous kindness to others, e.g. children who have been bullied, or feel sad.	Makes people feel welcome and respected in the classroom. Wants to make people feel better if they are sad or scared or have been bullied.	Makes others feel welcomed and respected at school. Uses a range of strategies for helping others.	Makes others feel valued and welcome in a range of contexts. Uses a range of strategies for helping others, and will actively tackle bullying/ stereotyping behaviours..
Relationship skills	**Foundation stage**	**Y1+2**	**Y3+4**	**Y5+6**
Group-working skills	Can share and work in a group, e.g. taking turns in a game; waiting his/her turn to say something; asking for help when stuck.	Can work well in a group. Can evaluate how well his/ her group have worked together.	Can take on a role in a group and contribute to the overall outcome helping others to reach a goal. Can evaluate how well a group is working together.	Can work well in a group, e.g. agreeing/ disagreeing assertively; listening to, and taking on board, constructive criticism. Can evaluate how well a group is working together. Demonstrates qualities of a good group leader.

Rights and personal/social responsibilities	Knows and keeps to routines and rules in the classroom.	Understands, contributes to, and keeps to rules in classroom.	Understands, contributes to, and keeps to rules in classroom, recognising his/her own and others' rights and responsibilities.	Understands, contributes to, and keeps to rules in school, recognising his/her own and others' rights and responsibilities, taking responsibility for his/her own behaviour.
Friendship	Plays well with other children, sharing toys and taking turns.	Knows what being a friend means. Can make and keep friends, using skills such as: • listening • giving compliments.	Can make and keep friends, using skills such as • using friendly behaviours • being a good listener • giving and receiving compliments.	Can make and keep friends at a variety of degrees of closeness. Does not see difference as a barrier to friendship. Is able to forgive others, and/or break the friendship as appropriate.
Assertiveness	Is able to say what he/she wants or needs.	Knows when and how to stand up for him/herself, and does so appropriately and without hurting others.	Uses assertiveness skills appropriately (including body language, tone, appropriate vocabulary).	Uses skills of assertiveness appropriately, e.g. • disagreeing with someone and accepting disagreement from others without falling out. • listening to others' views, but standing up for own viewpoint and making own choice, even if the majority viewpoint is different.

Problem-solving and conflict resolution	Can say sorry when he/she has been unkind or done something wrong. Can make up when he/she has fallen out with a friend.	Is able to apologise appropriately. Has strategies for making up with a friend, e.g. 'peaceful problem-solving.'	Is able to apologise appropriately and make amends when he/she has done something unkind. Can make up with a friend using e.g. 'peaceful problem-solving', showing understanding of the other person's point of view and seeking a 'win-win' solution.	Is able to apologise appropriately. Can make up with peers using e.g. 'peaceful problem-solving.' Can support others in solving their conflicts. Knows how to de-escalate a conflict (e.g. using 'I messages'; talking about the behaviour rather than the person).
Responsible decision making	**Foundation stage**	**Y1+2**	**Y3+4**	**Y5+6**
Goal-setting and planning/ review	Can set, work towards and achieve a self-selected immediate goal.	Can set, work towards and achieve a self-selected short-term goal, breaking it down into small steps.	Can set, work towards and achieve a self-selected medium-term goal, breaking it down into small steps, identifying and planning for obstacles, setting success criteria and evaluating outcomes and learning.	Can set, work towards and achieve a longer-term goal independently, breaking it down into small steps, identifying and planning for obstacles, setting success criteria and evaluating outcomes and learning.

Learning behaviours and skills: motivation focus persistence resilience	Understands that you have to work hard to achieve a goal. Can complete a task, focusing attention and concentrating appropriately.	Will work towards a reward, including the satisfaction of completing a task. Can usually resist distractions. Has some strategies for overcoming feelings of boredom and frustration.	Can motivate self to work. Can concentrate and resist distractions. Perseveres with a task. Manages frustration when tasks are difficult or boring. Can delay gratification.	Can motivate self to work. Can concentrate and resist distractions. Perseveres with a task. Manages frustration. Can delay gratification. Is willing to try again if he/she doesn't succeed.

Useful websites

These websites provide useful teaching resources for work on social and emotional learning.

- BBC Bitesize for animated films using puppets to explore a range of feelings and getting on with others:
  - www.bbc.co.uk/teach/class-clips-video/pshe-early-years-foundation-stage-ks1-feeling-better/zm2st39
  - www.bbc.co.uk/bitesize/subjects/zvryt39
  - www.bbc.co.uk/bitesize/topics/z478gwx/articles/zhhvpg8
- BBC Early Years collection: www.bbc.co.uk/teach/class-clips-video/pshe-early-years-foundation-stage-ks1-feeling-better/zm2st39
- BBC's emotional literacy series, including:
  - how the emotional brain can hijack the thinking brain: www.bbc.co.uk/programmes/p011sqwv
  - two films on anger: www.bbc.co.uk/programmes/p011nbvv and www.bbc.co.uk/programmes/p011l62c
  - seeing both sides of a story: www.bbc.co.uk/programmes/p011n8cj
  - working well in a team: www.bbc.co.uk/programmes/p011m8d9
- BBC's I-Player Lifebabble collection
  - www.bbc.co.uk/cbbc/shows/lifebabble
  - www.bbc.co.uk/cbbc/joinin/seven-times-you-had-to-bounce-back
  - www.bbc.co.uk/cbbc/thingstodo/mood-jar
- Class DoJo for managing moods and powerful emotions: https://ideas.classdojo.com/
- Empathy Lab for using books to develop empathy: www.empathylab.uk/
- Go Noodle for all sorts of short videos on emotions and self-regulation: www.gonoodle.com/tags/PXodv2/flow-and-steady?tab=videos
- Mood Meter: https://heartmindonline.org/resources/boost-emotional-intelligence-with-the-mood-meter
- Social and Emotional Aspects of Learning (SEAL): www.sealcommunity.org.uk, for a wide range of sequenced, age-related teaching and learning resources
- Sesame Street resources for EYFS and KS1, content on coping strategies:
  - https://sesamestreetincommunities.org/topics/traumatic-experiences/
  - https://sesamestreetincommunities.org/topics/caring/

References

Allen, R. (2020) *Pre-school to prison pipeline.* TED Talk. www.tedxmilehigh. com/preschool-to-prison-pipeline

Bates, A. (2021) *Self-regulation for staff and pupils.* Optimus Education blog. https://my.optimus-education.com/self-regulation-staff-and-pupils

Bates, A. (2022) *'Miss, I don't give a sh*t': Engaging with challenging behaviour in schools.* Thousand Oaks, CA: Corwin Ltd.

Brown, C. (2017) Research learning communities: How the RLC approach enables teachers to use research to improve their practice and the benefits for students that occur as a result. *Research for All*, 1(2), 387–405.

Caldarella, P., Larsen, R., Williams, L. et al. (2020) Effects of teachers' praise-to-reprimand ratios on elementary students' on-task behaviour. *Educational Psychology*, 40(10), 1306–11132.

CASEL (2020) *CASEL's SEL Framework.* https://casel.org/casel-sel-frame work-11-2020/

Chowdry, H. and McBride, T. (2017) *Disadvantage, behaviour and cognitive outcomes.* London: Early Intervention Foundation.

Desautels, L. (2019) *How teachers can help students co-regulate their emotions in the discipline process.* Edutopia blog, October 5. www.edu topia.org/article/role-emotion-co-regulation-discipline?fbclid=IwAR0TpC OCKkPaVA9VjSBHS-SVKk9MCsNdb3_TTgQYpRujcsR2RxRNjJ_XbTQ

Durlak, A., Dymnicki, A., Schellinger, K. and Weissberg, R. (2011) The impact of enhancing students' social and emotional learning: A meta-analysis of school-based universal interventions. *Child Development*, 82(1), 405–432.

Durlak, J., Mahoney, J. and Boyle, A. (2022) What we know, and what we need to find out about universal, school-based social and emotional learning programs for children and adolescents: A review of meta-analyses and directions for future research. *Psychological Bulletin*, 148(11–12), 765–782.

Gedikoglu, M. (2021) *Social and emotional learning: An evidence review and synthesis of key issues.* London: Education Policy Institute.

Godfrey, D. (2017) What is the proposed role of research evidence in England's 'self-improving' school system? *Oxford Review of Education*, 43(4), 433–446.

Gross, J. (2011) Character in education. Should character be 'taught' through the curriculum or 'caught' through a school's ethos? In Lexmond, J. and Grist, M. (Eds) *The character inquiry.* London: Demos.

Gross, J. (2021) *Reaching the unseen children: Practical strategies for closing stubborn gaps in disadvantaged groups.* Abingdon: Routledge.

Harper, L. (2016) Using picture books to promote social-emotional literacy. *Young Children*, 71 (3), 80–86.

Harvey, N. (2021) *Strategies to support anxiety.* https://blog.optimus-edu cation.com/strategies-support-anxiety

Heracleous, L. and Jacobs, C. (2008) Crafting strategy: The role of embodied metaphors. *Long Range Planning*, 41(3), 309–325.

Kuypers, L. (2021) *The Zones of Regulation: A curriculum designed to foster self-regulation and emotional control.* Santa Clara, CA: Think Social Publishing.

Nikolajeva, M. (2013) Picture books and emotional literacy. *International Reading Association*, 67(4), 249–254.

Otte, E. and Rousseau, R. (2002) Social network analysis: A powerful strategy, also for the information sciences. *Journal of Information Science*, 28(6), 441–453.

Perry, B. (2009) Speaking in a video. www.youtube.com/watch?v=ZVRO7 PdYRnM

Reinke, W., Herman, K. and Newcomer, L. (2016) The brief student-teacher classroom interaction observation. *Assessment for Effective Intervention*, 42(1), 32–42.

Rogers, E.M. (2003) *Diffusion of innovations* (5th edn). New York: Free Press.

Schiller, P. (2009) *Seven skills for school success: Activities to develop social and emotional intelligence in young children.* Beltsville, MD: Gryphon House.

Siegel, D. (2014) *Brainstorm: The power and purpose of the teenage brain.* London: Penguin Publishing Group.

Siegel, D.J. and Payne Bryson, T. (2011) *The whole-brain child: 12 revolutionary strategies to nurture your child's developing mind.* London: Bantam Books.

Taylor, R.D., Oberle, E., Durlak, J.A. and Weissberg, R.P. (2017) Promoting positive youth development through school-based social and emotional learning interventions: A meta-analysis of follow-up effects. *Child Development*, 88, 1156–1171.

Van Poortvliet, M., Clarke, A. and Gross, J. (2019) *Improving social and emotional learning in primary schools. Guidance report.* London: Education Endowment Foundation.

Index

Page numbers in *italics* refer to figures.

T - #0200 - 090625 - C180 - 297/210/9 - PB - 9781032500720 - Matt Lamination